THE
NAZIS
AND THE
OCCULT

THE
NAZIS
AND THE
OCCULT

DUSTY SKLAR

DORSET PRESS
New York

Grateful acknowledgment is due to the following for permission to quote material which appears in this book:

Grosset & Dunlap, Inc., for excerpts from "Psychotherapy and Political World View" by Kurt Gauger and "The Earth-Centered Jew Lacks a Soul" by Alfred Rosenberg, in *Nazi Culture* by George Mosse. Copyright © 1966 by Grosset & Dunlap, Inc. Used by permission of Grosset & Dunlap, Inc.

Harcourt Brace Jovanovich, Inc., for excerpts from *Hitler* by Joachim Fest.

Harper & Row, Publishers, Inc. for excerpts from *The True Believer*, by Eric Hoffer. Copyright 1951 by Eric Hoffer. Reprinted by permission of Harper & Row, Publishers, Inc.

Hoover Institution Press, for excerpts from *Heinrich Himmler: A Nazi in the Making* by Bradley F. Smith. Reprinted with the permission of the publishers, Hoover Institution Press. Copyright © 1971 by the board of trustees of the Leland Stanford Junior University.

Houghton Mifflin Company, for excerpts from *Mein Kampf*, by Adoplf Hitler, translated by Ralph Manheim, and *The Young Hitler I Knew*, by August Kubizek.

New American Library, for excerpts from *Prophecy in Our Time*, by Martin Ebon. Copyright by Martin Ebon.

The New Republic, for excerpts from "Is Hitler Youth Curable?", by Heinrich Fraenkel. Reprinted by permission of *The New Republic*, copyright 1944, The New Republic, Inc.

Pantheon Books, for excerpts from *The Face of the Third Reich*, by Joachim Fest. Copyright © 1970 by Weidenfield & Nicolson, Ltd. Reprinted by permission of Pantheon Books, a division of Random House, Inc.

Princeton University Press, for excerpts from *Political Violence Under the Swastika: 581 Early Nazis*, by Peter H. Merkl. Copyright © 1975 by Princeton University Press. For excerpts from *C. G. Jung: Letters, 1: 1906-1950*, edited by Gerhard Adler, in collaboration with Aniela Jaffe, Bollingen Series XCV. Copyright © 1973 by Princeton University Press. Reprinted by permission of Princeton University Press.

G. P. Putnam's Sons, for excerpts from *Zodiac and Swastika*, by Wilhelm Wulff and *The Voice of Destruction*, by Hermann Rauschning.

The University of Chicago Press, for excerpts from *They Thought They Were Free*, by Milton Mayer. Copyright 1955 by The University of Chicago. All rights reserved.

Originally published under the title *Gods and Beasts: The Nazis and the Occult*.

This edition published by Dorset Press, a division of Marboro Books Corporation, by arrangement with Dusty Sklar.
1989 Dorset Press

133

ISBN 0-88029-412-4
(formerly ISBN 0-690-01232-2)

SKLAR

Printed in the United States of America

M 9 8 7

1542069

*For my mother and father
and for Dave, Steve, Lisa, and Joe*

Contents

Acknowledgments

In preparing this book, I have drawn on a wide variety of sources. The bibliography should not be taken as representing the whole of my source material, but rather as a list of suggestions for further reading.

I owe a special debt of gratitude to my husband, David, and my son, Steven, for their encouragement.

Hugh Rawson, my editor, performed the weary task of scrutinizing the manuscript.

Translation assistance was given by Hans Karlsruher.

It is not possible for me to thank all of the members (enchanted and disenchanted) of esoteric groups in America and England for information given in a spirit of cooperation and with a desire to enlarge our understanding of an emotionally charged, controversial subject.

. . . being frequently driven into straits where rules are useless, and being often kept fluctuating pitiably between hope and fear by the uncertainty of fortune's greedily coveted favors, they are consequently, for the most part, very prone to credulity. The human mind is readily swayed this way or that in times of doubt, especially when hope and fear are struggling for the mastery. . . .

. . . in adversity they know not where to turn, but beg and pray for counsel from every passer-by. No plan is then too futile, too absurd, or too fatuous for their adoption. . . .

—Spinoza

THE
NAZIS
AND THE
OCCULT

CHAPTER I

Hidden Roots

Real power begins where secrecy begins . . . the only rule
of which everybody in a totalitarian state may be sure.

Hannah Arendt

Many books have been written about Hitler and the Holocaust, many reasons suggested to account for them. It is said that Germany in the 1930's was economically and spiritually bankrupt, that Hitler and his henchmen were madmen or simple opportunists or petty bureaucrats—or some combination of the three. Perhaps. But one explanation tends to contradict another, and when all are combined, they merge into a solution so general that nothing is explained. Understandably, then, many people are still not satisfied that the grotesque events of the Third Reich have been adequately dealt with by the historians.

In all this complicated story, there is one question which cries out for an answer: How is it that the theorists have missed a vital element, even when they themselves provide important clues? That element is the occult.

Many historians have alluded to the Nazi party's origins in an occult sect, to the occult leanings of leading Nazi officials, to the mystical rites of the SS and the Hitler Youth, to the establishment of a bureau devoted exclusively to the occult during World War II. It now seems puzzling that they should not also have given as much consideration to the underlying basis for these odd phenomena as they gave to economic and social factors. That they did not is, of course, evidence of their own dismissal—quite

1

reasonably—of a crankish pseudoscience. But this has led, inevitably, to selective blindness. In order not to be accused of giving credence to irrational beliefs, they have failed to see those beliefs in their proper historical perspective. Since early studies always influence later ones, the interpretation of Nazi origins has tended to remain pretty much the same for the past two decades.

All the same, people do seem to have a subliminal awareness that the Nazis were involved in occultism. One often comes across references such as these: "The Nazi horror . . . reveals how Satanic the human soul can become." "If there is anything fundamentally diabolic about [Anton] LaVey, it stems . . . from the echo of nazism in his theories. . . ." "It was predictable that [Charles] Manson would identify with Hitler, for they [both] have been motivated by a kindred demonic spirit and they are comparable personalities."

The current occult revival has placed us in a better position to examine the Nazi horror from a different perspective, and gives ample ground for believing that occult beliefs and practices, however weird, played a major part in the irrational history of the Third Reich.

Some scholars may have been thrown off the scent because Hitler went to great pains to eradicate occultism from Germany almost as soon as he came to power, and on that account, is mistakenly identified as an enemy of irrational faith.

On the contrary. As will be borne out in later chapters, the occult was purged, not because it was abhorrent, but because the Nazis took it seriously—so seriously, indeed, that it posed a potential threat. The astrologer William Wulff, who was put to work by the SS casting horoscopes of nations, groups, and movements, describes, in *Zodiac and Swastika*, Heinrich Himmler's confession of his own interest in and practice of occultism and his explanation of the purge:

> For us politics means . . . the elimination of all forces except those serving the one constructive idea. . . .
> In the Third Reich we have to forbid astrology. . . . We cannot permit any astrologers to follow their calling except those who are working for us. In the National Socialist state astrology must remain a *privilegium singulorum*. It is not for the broad masses.

The Holocaust appeared in a new light when I began, some time ago, to investigate certain modern esoteric cults making claims to paranormal knowledge. These cults, from those connected with George Ivanovitch Gurdjieff, Madame Helena Petrovna Blavatsky, and Rudolf Steiner to their present reincarnations, shared certain features: an authoritarian obedience to a charismatic and Messianic leader; secrecy; loyalty to the group above all other ties; a belief in supernatural possibilities open to the members only; a belief in reincarnation; initiation into superhuman sources of power; literal acceptance of the myth of ancient "giants" or supermen who handed down an oral tradition to a chosen people and who were guiding us now; and, in uncommon cases, Satanic practices.

Glaring parallels to Nazi history. Turning back to that history and its antecedents, I saw unmistakable evidence of a direct relationship between the Nazis and occultism. In fact, it was hard *not* to see it. Here was the missing link in our understanding of the beasts who proclaimed themselves gods.

If it seems too fantastic to believe that one of the most civilized countries in the world should have fallen to occultism, here is a highly respected German historian, an exiled former staff member of the liberal newspaper *Frankfurter Zeitung*, Konrad Heiden, observing, in his introduction to *The Memoirs of Dr. Felix Kersten*, Heinrich Himmler's masseur, that among the Germans

the best of them found refuge from the despair of their daily life in a perverse fanaticism . . . called "the mysticism of a political movement."

Germany was the perfect place for this development. In almost no other country were so many "miracles" performed, so many ghosts conjured, so many illnesses cured by magnetism, so many horoscopes read, between the two World Wars. A veritable mania of superstition had seized the country, and all those who made a living by exploiting human stupidity thought the millennium had come. General [Erich] Ludendorff, who had commanded the German armies in World War I, tried to make gold with the assistance of a swindler boasting the appropriate name of *Tausend* (meaning "thousand"). There was scarcely a folly in natural or world history to which the great general did not lend credence; when the German Republic, which he hated so intensely, had the barriers of the railway crossings painted red and white for better visibility, Ludendorff declared that the Jews in the government were doing this because Moses had led the Jews through the desert under these colors.

Another high-ranking general was convinced that he possessed the secret of the death ray and that he could halt airplanes in their flight and stop tanks in their tracks. A steamship company dismissed its managing director because his handwriting had displeased a graphologist. Motorists avoided a certain road between Hamburg and Bremen because, it was rumored, from milestone number 113 there emanated certain mysterious "terrestrial rays," which provoked one accident after another. A miracle worker, who had the faculty of making the dead Bismarck appear during his mass meetings and who healed the sick by application of white cheese, had enough followers to establish a city; another crackpot was almost elected to the Reichstag; and still a third, who also barely missed election, promised to perform the greatest miracle of all by undoing the German inflation that had depreciated the mark to the value of one trillion paper marks for one gold mark.

Among Hitler's intimates was a man on whose visiting card appeared the word "magician" to indicate his profession—and he meant it in all seriousness. Many were convinced that the course of world history was the sinister result of the ministrations of ancient secret societies—as such they considered not only the Free Masons, but also Jews and the Jesuits. . . .

Other historians have corroborated that Germany between the two world wars was particularly ripe for these states of mind. It was a time of alienation and impotence. World War I had turned everything inside out. Apart from the physical devastations, the three bugbears of taxation, inflation, and confiscation sapped the strength of the middle class. The war itself was but a symptom of growing inner turbulence in Europe. The trouble had, of course, begun much earlier. In Germany particularly, the gap between an advancing technology and an outmoded social order was great.

In the years preceding World War I, the German Jews were in an especially vulnerable position. The full emancipation of the German Jews, which had come in 1871, brought large numbers of Eastern European Jews to Germany. They settled in the cities, taking a prominent part in commercial, cultural, and political life. Likewise, the period from 1857 to 1910 saw a rise in the Jewish population of Vienna of more than 400 percent. Because of the high value the Jews placed on learning, a disproportionately large number went into the medical and legal professions, trying in that way to gain a modicum of social acceptance. Some Germans, of course, mistook these professionals for the average Jew. Slowly, a new religion evolved for those Germans who felt somehow cheated—a cult of race, based on the supremacy of the Aryans and the vilification of the Jews. It was called the *völkisch*—or Pan-German—movement, and it enjoyed great popular appeal. It began a virulent campaign against the "foreign element." A racial theory of history was developed, and it heralded the coming of a new Messiah. The mystical concepts of *Reich* and *Volk* went along with an awakening interest in occultism. Secret cults sprang up, anti-Semitic and nationalistic, running like a sewer beneath Vienna and other cultural centers.

Two Austrian occultists, Jörg Lanz von Liebenfels and Guido von List, presented an irrational, pseudo-anthropological package which attracted a number of wealthy backers, despite its foolishness. Lanz's Order of New Templars and List's Armanen boasted several influential members.

In 1909, young Adolf Hitler, down and out in Vienna, came across Lanz's magazine, *Ostara*, and made contact with the occultist. The erotic language and racist rantings of this magazine were remarkably similar to Hitler's later utterances.

Membership in occult groups was often interlocking. When, in 1912, a new secret cult, the Germanen Orden, was born, disciples of both Lanz and List joined. The Germanen Orden was like the other occult-racist-nationalist groups, but with a difference. It called for "courageous men" to "accomplish the work" of combating the Social Democrats, who had gained ground in the elections of 1912. Courageous men did not leap forth to join the Germanen Orden, but after World War I prospects were brighter.

People were in a state of shock over the German defeat, which had brought with it the collapse of Kaiser Wilhelm II's regime. Power was suddenly thrust into the hands of a provisional democratic government whose unenviable task it was to accept the consequences of a lost war, reluctantly surrender, and sign a peace treaty. Extremists of the left and right blamed everything on this government: Germany's humiliation, as well as the reparations which bore heavily, financially and psychologically, on the people. It was the end of an era. The Germans had gone into the war with such high hopes. The war was to have been a release from care, a cleansing of mounting economic and social problems, a purging and purification. When the war began, said one German, "it was as if a nightmare had vanished, as if a door had opened, and an old yearning had been satisfied." The idea of war itself had become beautiful. It was to give people back their lives. "Peace," as someone pointed out, "had become insupportable." Hitler embodied the alienated man with no family or occupation, to whom the outbreak of World War I was a godsend. He later confessed: "For me, as for every German, there now began the greatest and most unforgettable time of my earthly existence."

When the Germans signed the peace treaty, the army released almost a quarter of a million men to add their numbers to the growing ranks of the unemployed. Many soldiers were dazed to come home to a fatherland on the edge of anarchy, hungry, and undisciplined. The new Russian Revolution threatened to spill over into Germany. In Munich, particularly, Communists stalked the streets, threatening civil war. Conservatives and liberals alike were anxious to do anything to stave off communism.

The Germanen Orden was happy to merge its destiny with a Munich group called the Thule Society, which was meeting regularly to study the supposed occult meaning of the ancient Germanic alphabet and its symbolism. It was led by an astrologer who called himself Baron Rudolf von Sebottendorff. The Thule Society soon became the political arm of the Germanen Orden and quietly set about preparing for a counterrevolution against the government. It formed an umbrella for many of the racist-nationalist groups and enlisted frightened or unscrupulous men against the government, which, it said, had betrayed the German people. In addition to rabid anti-Semitism, it preached the coming of a *Führer* who would do away with hated democracy, the handmaiden of the weak. It began to collect weapons, bought a newspaper, instigated terrorist activity and stirred up race hatred against the Jews, all the while keeping up the front of being a study group for Germanic antiquity. Thule members who were to play key roles in the formation of the Nazi party were Alfred Rosenberg, Rudolf Hess, Gottfried Feder, Karl Harrer, and Dietrich Eckart. Not until they found their Führer, Adolf Hitler, were they able to carry out the irrational programs of Lanz, List, and Sebottendorff. But all the essential ingredients—the ideology, the rituals, the symbols, the attitudes—of the coming Nazi Revolution were already present in the Germanen Orden and the Thule Society, as well as the Order of the New Templars and the Armanen.

CHAPTER 2

Giants in the Earth

There were giants in the earth in those days. . . .

—Genesis 6:4

German occult groups did not appear out of nowhere. They had historical antecedents. The new Aryan hero trumpeted by List and Lanz owed his birth to the unholy marriage of early Hindu ideas of racial purity and Darwin's concept of evolution, which was consummated in the nineteenth-century Europe where German romantics, in particular, were fascinated with racial theories.

The nineteenth century was remarkable for great change. In Germany the change was more drastic than in the rest of Europe. Its people had been more completely under the sway of the past; the Middle Ages had still been dominant in agriculture and industry. The Thirty Years' War, which began in 1618, had consolidated land holdings into fewer and fewer hands, and the land reforms which followed only served to crush the people lower down on the social scale. The industrial revolution happened more rapidly in Germany than anywhere else. It went from mining 1.5 million metric tons of coal in 1850, for instance, to 30 million in 1871. From a backward, predominantly agricultural country, it grew almost overnight into a modern industrial state, much as Japan and Sweden did in the twentieth century. Mass migrations of people from country to city severed traditional ties. Scientific discovery brought a sharp decline in religious faith, and there was a search for new values with which to identify. The state, assuming more and more control, seemed bent on crushing individuality. The European romantics, wincing at the bitter fruits of modern "progress," delighted in the exoticisms of the East. European rule in the Orient, travel, and translations of the Oriental classics helped lift the veils from the faces of the ancient Eastern civilizations. What the Europeans caught a glimpse of was a kind of serenity which had disappeared from the West and which was very much desired. So great was the Eastern influence that Victor Hugo observed in 1829: "In the age of Louis XIV, all the world was Hellenist; now it is orientalist."

Napoleon's army, entering Egypt in 1798, found the Rosetta Stone, which scholars labored to decipher. When Champollion solved the riddle, the long-lost tongue of that ancient civilization was loosened and the way opened for the great achievements of the modern science of Egyptology. German archaeologists went along with the Prussian king's expedition in 1842 and further refined the study.

The Germans also made important contributions to understanding the real nature of Islamic literature and thought. Persian love poems, called *ghazals*, had the greatest effect on German poets. The most brilliant of the Persian poems were Sufi. In the Sufi tradition, the poems were interpreted as allegorical and mystical revelations of the divine. German poet-scholars made use of them to such an extent that Heinrich Heine admonished: "These poor poets eat too freely of the fruit they steal from the garden groves of Shiraz, and then they vomit *ghazals*."

The Muslims had prejudiced the Europeans against the Hindus, whom they regarded as superstitious and degraded. But with the translation of ancient Sanskrit texts, India began to exert a fascination on the West.

The philosopher Johann Gottfried von Herder read Indian philosophy with enthusiasm and managed to inspire the German romantics, who were markedly different from the romantics in Europe at large—more given to morbid bitterness. Herder cautioned them not to be frightened by supernatural elements such as gods moving among men or nature personified. These, he said, were depictions of actual experiences, for on that paradisical river, the Ganges, the golden age still existed. The romantics could not have been more pleased, longing as they were for just such a golden age. "It is to the East," wrote Friedrich Schlegel in 1800, "that we must look for the supreme Romanticism."

A French version of the Upanishads awakened Arthur Schopenhauer to the wisdom of the East. His pessimistic view of a demonic will, blind and insatiable, compelling all things to share in its own futile unrest, had a tremendous influence on German thought, falling in with the disappointed mood of the age. Schopenhauer's sterile negation of life was soon imitated by like minds. The cessation of activity, for the sake of eventual purification, had a definite appeal for tired, hopeless people who could now enjoy renunciation under the cloak of Orientalism. The historian Benedetto Croce observed that this often led to a "sad and bitter sensuality, of decay and death . . . tinged with Satanism and sadism."

The spiritual journey to the East, undertaken by many German scholars, philosophers, and men of letters, brought a new mythology to a politically, economically, and socially despairing country: a mystical view that all finitude is the result of a fall from the absolute and that the effects of the Fall have to be repaired by the course of history. These writers began to glorify the Middle Ages as a period of dialogue with God, when men, art, and religion had been unified. To restore the lost innocence became their aim.

Asia's effect on the West took a terrible turn when the ancient Hindu doctrine of the race purity of the ruling class was rationalized by the Germans to demonstrate Aryan superiority over the Jews. In the mid-1800's, German philologists had theorized that their noble Aryan forebears in India had the same mystical symbols and gods as the ancient Germans. A French diplomat and Orientalist, Arthur de Gobineau, made race the determining characteristic in the rise and fall of civilizations. Gobineau's theory was that the racially pure Aryans were bastardized by alien racial elements, producing, by the process of civilization, a decadent people. It was the Semites, he said, hybridized by blacks, who were responsible for the Fall.

Gobineau's work not only gave an air of pseudo-respectability to the budding anti-Semitism in Germany, it provided a convenient rationale for the economic and social fall of the nobleman—for his failure to return to paradise. Even the caste system in India, he claimed, had not been sufficiently stringent to protect the ruling elite from the defiling blood of the dark-skinned races they had subjugated. His ideas penetrated throughout Germany. The German romantics, given a shot in the arm by Gobineau, could now view themselves as a natural aristocracy replacing the older, outmoded feudal aristocracy, which no longer accorded well with the idea of progress. After all, the Teutons, whom Gobineau equated with the Aryans, were the superior race. This idea was eagerly seized on and was buttressed by the growing resentment against the Jews.

In the early nineteenth century, the Jews had begun to move toward

equality and citizenship in Germany. Before then, the mass of them lived in
ghettos behind walls, were taxed heavily, and were barred from any work
but peddling and petty trade except for a select few, and even then under
prohibitions which gave them a bare subsistence. Even the more fortunate,
like the philosopher Moses Mendelssohn, at the height of his fame in 1776,
reported that to enter Dresden he was forced to pay "a head tax" equivalent
to that set for "a Polish cow."

Ludwig Boerne, a satirist born in 1786, writing of his boyhood
memories in a Frankfurt ghetto, recalls:

> There they rejoiced in the tender watchful care of the government. On
> Sundays they were prohibited from leaving the ghetto lane, to spare
> them from being beaten up by drunkards. Before the age of twenty-five
> they were forbidden to marry, in order that their offspring prove sound
> and sturdy. On public holidays they had to reenter the ghetto gate by
> sharp six in the evening, lest over-exposure to the sun ruin their com-
> plexions. They were forbidden to stroll in the fields beyond the city wall,
> so as to run no risk of being attracted to the life of a farmer. When a Jew
> walked the city streets and a Christian cried *Mach Mores, Jud!* ("Your
> manners, Jew!"), he needs must remove his hat; in this way the proper
> politeness was maintained between the two faiths. Then, too, a great
> many of the streets—their bumpy pavement was bad for the feet—were
> altogether closed to him.

After the German emancipation of the Jews, which took several decades
to complete, there was a huge influx of Jews from the Eastern European
countries, which were still guilty of fierce persecutions. Life in Germany
was more hospitable to them. But in time, the majority of Germans,
scratching out a bare living themselves, began to resent them. Boerne
understood well the hostility of these Germans, who flattered themselves
that no matter how low their estate, they were at least not members of an
inferior race:

> The poor Germans! Living in the lowest floor, oppressed by the seven
> floors of the upper classes, their anxiety is made lighter by speaking of
> people who are still lower than they are and who live in the cellar. Not
> being a Jew provides them with consolation at not being a state
> councillor.

Gobineau became the prophet for all these "poor Germans" and provided them with a philosophy which preached the nobility of the Aryan by simple virtue of his birth. From this eminent source they learned that contamination of race would lead to the certain decline of Germany.

The growing völkisch movement began an active battle against the Jews, the defilers of their blood, reinforced by a pseudo-scholarly writer who satisfied their desire for academic respectability. Rightist Pan-German groups also bolstered their ideology by citing the dubious philosophical, historical, and scientific analyses laid out by Houston Stewart Chamberlain, an Englishman in love with German culture.

Though painfully dull, his two-volume *Foundations of the Nineteenth Century*, published in 1900, had a strange appeal. He told a mass society, at the mercy of the impersonal forces which were crushing it, that the Teutons were indomitable master builders, that in mysticism was freedom, that "every Mystic is, whether he will or not, a born Anti-Semite," and that Darwin's theory of natural selection justifies the stricture against mingling of the races.

Even before Chamberlain, völkisch thinkers had tried to weave together lessons from history proving the heroism of the ancient Germanic past. Many of them were admirers of the Theosophical Society, which combined for the first time certain elements into a cohesive system considered by some people to be the beginning of modern occultism.

The Theosophical Society was organized in New York City in 1875 by Madame Helena Petrovna Blavatsky, a Russian expatriate countess known to her disciples as H. P. B. At seventeen, her family had forced her to marry an elderly Russian general, whom she promptly deserted. Headstrong, convinced that she had mediumistic powers, and versed in many languages, she wandered about Europe and the East, and decided at age forty to come to New York to investigate spiritualism, which had become an American craze. Her mission, a Society historian observed, was "to explain its phenomena, expose its frauds, to enlarge its spiritual scope, and to give it the dignity in the world of science which was its due." Depleted of financial resources, if not of energy, she delivered up an unlikely package of Hinduism, Gnosticism, and pseudoscience which had a tremendous impact on the intelligentsia of the West. She even converted the Indians themselves to the "ancient wisdom" in modern dress. Her ideas, about ancient lost races with secret knowledge of the ultimate nature of reality, the immortal soul perfecting itself through endless rebirths, and mastery of superhuman powers which could unlock the secrets of the universe, if they had been presented by traditional organized religions, would not have been credited. But people were perfectly willing to suspend disbelief of a huge Russian countess with magnetic eyes who smoked cigars and used bawdy language.

Darwin's *Origin of Species*, published in 1859, had widened the chasm between science and religion. H. P. B. leaped across that chasm with a spiritual concept of evolution. Men could become divine, she said, by advancing in an evolutionary process which was part of an elaborate cosmology affecting whole races.

It was possible to thwart evolution, however. Like most occultists, she believed in the old Gnostic doctrine that there were two worlds, one good and one evil.

In Gnostic thinking, spirit and matter were opposed to each other, matter being an interruption of the order of the cosmos—a fall, and therefore evil. The Gnostics posited three classes: spiritual, or pneumatic, men; animal, or psychic, men; and carnal, or physical, men. The last were said to be wholly material and could not be saved, their nature being evil; they had not a single spark of the divine in them.

Matter, according to the Gnostics, was not the creation of the supreme god but of a demiurge, an inferior divinity. A famous medieval Gnostic sect, the Cathars, came to identify the Old Testament god, Jehovah, with the demiurge, the creator of the material world, and therefore the equivalent of Satan. Within Gnosticism, then, existed the idea that the Jewish god was really the devil, responsible for all the evil in the world.

Without intending to arouse hatred against the Jews, H. P. B. repeated this Gnostic thinking in her book *The Secret Doctrine*:

With the Semite, that *stooping* man meant the *fall* of Spirit into matter, and that *fall* and *degradation* were apotheosized by him with the result of dragging Deity down to the level of man. . . . The Aryan views of the symbolism were those of the whole Pagan world; the Semite interpretations emanated from and were pre-eminently those of a small tribe, thus marking its national features and the idiosyncratic defects that characterize many of the Jews to this day—gross realism, selfishness, and sensuality. [Italics hers.]

She talked of a race of giants that existed in ancient days and argued that the occasional appearance of giants in modern times proved that species tend to revert to the original type. She held that since the days of the giants, whose descendants the Aryans were, there had been an unbroken succession of semi-immortal "adepts" living in secret cities in Tibetan mountains. It was *they* who had appointed her as their emissary.

Because of the flamboyance of her personality, if not her prose, H. P. B. became the model for other aspiring occultist leaders. She had somehow managed to make magic, witchcraft, and alchemy respectable. With the support of educated people, her ideas spread. She brought to the last decades of the nineteenth century a universal palliative for the materialism from which it was suffering.

The völkisch writers made capital of both Theosophy and Darwinism. Darwin's book had been hailed in Germany with an acclamation in startling contrast to the storm of protest which greeted it elsewhere. In place of a dogmatic Christian theology preaching a millennium, there came a conviction that human society was moving blindly toward some ideal goal. The struggle for existence, palpable to every German, justified itself in this evolutionary scheme of nature. *Origin of Species* sold briskly in Germany. The Germans eagerly pressed Darwin with their own writings on the subject, lauding his work. It was said that although Darwin was English, Darwinism really came into its own in Germany. As one German scientist pointed out: "You are still discussing in England whether or not the theory of Darwin can be true. We have got a long way beyond that stage here. His theory is now our common starting point."

To a growing body of anthropological concepts was now fused the idea that the *karma* of the Aryans was to engage in a race struggle to the death against the Jews. Germans, the fittest to survive, were destined to become the saviors of the human race. For this, Gúido von List preached, they would need a "strong man from above," who would be reincarnated from an ancient soldier. List's study of the origins of Jewish mysticism had taught him the importance of imbuing a people with a Messianic hope. When the world is changing and the old knowledge becomes suspect, it is necessary to herald the coming of a Messiah so that the traditional verities may be adapted to new conditions. List gave the Germans, in effect, an opportunity to become competitors of the Jews for the honor of "chosen people." His secular Messianic nationalism was taken seriously by many confused apostles. The German people were to take their place at the head of all nations, act as their leader, and move them toward civilization. *They* were the chosen people, and soon a Führer would arise among them who, in turn, would lead the Messianic nation.

Just before World War I, then, side by side with an awakening interest in occultism went an interest in racist-nationalism. Germany's supremacy was "proved" by the ideas and events of the distant past, when the Teutons lived close to nature and far from modern artificiality. The call of the elemental, the breath of the woodland, the simple poetry of *Wanderlust*, of joyous roving, asserted themselves. The folktales and folk songs issuing from the lips of peasants became sacred. Primitive German institutions and folklore were eagerly studied. Whereas, for primitive peoples, nature often represented primordial chaos, and therefore the enemy, these neo-primitives idealized nature and anathematized the city as profane, an aberrant discovery of modern man in his wickedness. Imagination, feeling, and will attributed to Natural Man, were placed above reason, which was held responsible for the psychic disorders of civilized man. The irrational was recognized as a source of illumination. List and his Theosophical friends claimed to have a "secret science" by which they could intuit the past and divine its meaning. Through extrasensory powers, they could communicate with the ghosts which hovered around ancient soil and in the cracks of ancient buildings. Innocent and pastoral at first, this movement back to nature and simplicity gradually grew more and more patriotic, more and more "German," to the exclusion of other races, and more and more anti-Semitic.

Both the occult and the racist-nationalist movements were hostile to modernity. Both promised a millennium. If all the former were not anti-Semitic, all the latter were. They saw in the Jew the exemplar of the modern man: urban, alienated from the soil, materialistic. Both movements were essentially conservative, in that they harked back to a golden age. The groups often intertwined. Under the influence of List and Lanz, whose works they studied, völkisch youth groups pressed for the expulsion of Jews from their organizations, from university life, and from the government. Admirers and disciples of both men became agitators for a final solution to the Jewish problem. Some saw that solution only in extermination.

Both also hailed the Middle Ages with uncritical admiration. Whereas the rest of Europe tended to brand that period as an era of darkness from which it had been happy to emerge, and to hold up the Renaissance as worthy of adoration, Germans idealized the Middle Ages as the most illustrious period of their history. The hierarchic structure of medieval society appealed to their longing for political security. Their morbid worship of the twelfth-century German Crusaders, the Order of Teutonic

Knights, for instance, was based on its mystical hierarchical structure, its secrecy, and its supernatural claims to world domination. Indeed, according to some people, the "thousand-year conspiracy" of conquest which the Teutonic Knights had threatened did persist into the twentieth century.

The marriage of occultism and nationalism is not as uneasy as it might appear on the surface. Each represents a nostalgia for a lost paradisical state, and a commitment to restoring that state in some millennial time. It is natural for people who feel uncertain about the future to look back sentimentally to a glorified past which they will try to relive. The Irish Theosophist William Sharp (who also wrote under the name Fiona MacLeod) was a nationalist-occultist who understood the connection between the patriotic longing and the longing for the occult:

I think our people have most truly loved their land, and their country, and their songs, and their ancient traditions, and that the word of bitterest savour is that sad word exile. But it is also true that in love we love vaguely another land, a rainbow-land, and that our most desired country is not the real Ireland, the real Scotland, the real Brittany, but the vague Land of Youth, the shadowy Land of Heart's Desire. And it is also true, that deep in the songs we love above all other songs is a lamentation for what is gone away from the world, rather than merely from us as a people: or a sighing of longing for what the heart desires but no mortal destiny requites.

It is not at all unusual to find such feelings of *Weltschmerz* in those periods when reason seems to have failed us and death and disorder wait to swallow us up. At such times, an interest in the occult gains ground steadily and tries to reintegrate the shattered cosmos.

This was the climate in Germany before World War I, and the war intensified it.

CHAPTER 3

Gods and Beasts

Gods and beasts, that is what our world is made of.

—Hitler, quoted in *The Voice of Destruction*
by *Hermann Rauschning*

In the years preceding World War I, German anti-Semitism was fed by an underground stream of secret cults running like a sewer beneath Vienna and other cultural centers. Hitler dipped into this stream. He lived in a flophouse in the city's slum area, and his life had all the elements of a scenario for a Charlie Chaplin movie about the Little Tramp. He was twenty when he came to Vienna in 1909, rejected for admission to the Academy of Fine Arts, and according to eyewitness accounts, lonely, shy with women, moody, given to violent outbursts—in short, even in those squalid quarters where the struggle for existence must have brought out the brutal side of human nature, exceedingly odd. He later wrote in *Mein Kampf* of this period that it gave him "the foundations of a knowledge" which sustained him for the rest of his life: "In this period there took shape within me a world picture and a philosophy which became the granite foundation of all my acts. In addition to what I then created, I have had to learn little; and I have had to alter nothing."

He spent much of his time studying Eastern religions, yoga, occultism, hypnotism, astrology, telepathy, graphology, phrenology, and similar subjects which often appeal to pursuers of magical powers, who usually happen to be powerless. His penchant for the occult led him to a tobacconist's shop near his lodging where he came upon a magazine, *Ostara*, which must have drawn him. This strange publication was produced by the mystical theorist, Lanz, who wrote under the acronyn PONT (Prior of the Order of the New Templars).

Vienna, in those days one of the fastest-growing cities in Europe, was hospitable to the formation of occult groups which sprang up with religious fervor, symptomatic of the irrational atmosphere of the time. Vienna's population went up 259 percent between 1860 and 1900, and the flood of new arrivals sought relief from the frustrations of an overcrowded and expensive existence. The city was deluged by mediums, necromancers, and astrologers who claimed to be occupied with a futuristic science which the scientific establishment was as yet unable to appreciate, since experiments were still unverified. The gullible—scholars included—believed that intuition and vision enabled specially endowed natures to investigate phenomena which eluded ordinary people.

Lanz, a defrocked Cistercian monk, started his group, the Order of the New Templars, in 1900. His friend, Guido von List, a somewhat different sort of pseudo-priest, started his group, the Armanen, in 1908. Membership was often interlocking, and there was continual feedback between the cults. Around 1912, a number of members of both cults finally came together under one roof in the Germanen Orden, which prefigured the Nazi party.

Historians are divided on the question of whether Hitler was actually ever a member of either the Temple of the New Order or the Armanen, but it is certain that he was a reader of *Ostara* and met Lanz several times in that period he later alluded to as providing him with "the foundations of a knowledge" which was to become so important to him.

Writing in an oracular, pseudo-anthropological manner, Lanz took mankind from the beginning of time and divided the species into the ace-men and the ape-men, the first being white, blue-eyed, blond, and responsible for everything heroic in mankind. The second group was the repository of everything vile. According to this comic-book mentality, the heroes—called variously *Asings, Heldinge*, or *Arioheroiker*—were superior by reason of breeding and blood, whereas the inferiors—*Afflinge, Waninge, Schrättlinge*, or *Tschandale*—always threatened to contaminate through interbreeding.

Ostara was one of a number of magazines which surfaced during this period. Like some of our own pulp magazines, it combined the erotic and the occult in an irrational blend which could capture the fantasies of lost

souls. Its lurid stories were calculated to explain history as a struggle to the
death between the pure Aryan and the hairy subhuman. This racial struggle, described in mystical, turgid prose, was the essence of human existence. To illustrate it, Lanz filled his pages with gorgeous blond women
falling into the snares of satyr-like men. For all the Aryan's superiority, it
was quite evident that there was one way in which he was not superior:
sexual prowess. The female member of the master race was sexual enough,
to be sure, but the male could not hope to compete against the enemy in
having sufficient potency to satisfy the infinite needs of the blond beauty. If
this sounds reminiscent of the Ku Klux Klan's pronouncements against the
"inferior" blacks, it is: The lower races must not pollute, through interbreeding, the rich blood of the higher races. Since, sexually, the lower
races are more potent, this presents a considerable challenge to the hero.

Lanz was writing in the tradition of a völkisch revival of the conservative
Germanic ideal of woman as the keeper of the hearth, in contrast with the
modern suffragette who was just then demanding her rights and asserting
her own sexual needs.

Race, blood, and sex combined with ancient German occultism—spells,
number mysticism—to make an overrich Viennese pastry. Not many
soup-kitchen derelicts, seeking an escape from their hopeless state, could
resist such a package. *Ostara, Briefbücherei der blonden Mannesrechtler*
("Newsletters of the Blond Fighters for the Rights of Men") addressed
these men, for example, in its March 1908 issue when it ran a full-page
advertisement promoting a book to help young men choose a career.
"What shall I become?" read the advertisement.

It is all too clear what one regular reader, Hitler, became, though the
direct influence of *Ostara* upon him is not known. His obsession with the
"nightmare vision of the seduction of hundreds and thousands of girls by
repulsive, bandy-legged Jew bastards" is identical with *Ostara*'s. We
have Hitler's own confession that one of his favorite movies was *King
Kong*, the plot of which might have been concocted by Lanz himself.

For such mentalities, *Ostara* was thoughtful enough to provide a yard-
stick by which the reader could measure himself as to racial worth and be
assured that he was not Jewish. The *Rassenwertigkeitindex* allowed him to
score on the basis of eye, hair, and skin color, and the size and shape of
nose, hands, feet, skull, and even buttocks. Black eyes were twelve points
to the bad, blue-gray eyes twelve points to the good. Being a reader of
Ostara was already sufficient qualification for membership in the "mixed

type," the stratum above the lower races. Hitler presumably would have rated himself in this category.

With headlines like these—ARE YOU BLOND? THEN YOU ARE THE CREATOR AND PRESERVER OF CIVILIZATION. ARE YOU BLOND? THEN YOU ARE THREATENED BY PERILS. READ THE LIBRARY FOR BLONDS AND ADVOCATES OF MALE RIGHTS.—and subtitles like these—Race and Nobility; Race and Foreign Affairs; The Metaphysics of Race—*Ostara*, thirty-five pfennigs a copy, sometimes reached circulation figures of 100,000 in Austria and Germany.

The Order of the New Templars which this ludicrous oracle founded enrolled blond, blue-eyed members—and only if they promised to marry women with the same attributes. This was of paramount importance, even though it would not guarantee race purity, since "Through woman, sin came into the world, and it so over and over again because woman is especially susceptible to the love artifices of her animal-like inferiors." The blond Siegfried must win her away from the dark seducer, slaying dragons and giants if necessary. Our interest in this theology is enriched on learning that Lanz's New Templars were assembled as soon as he himself was expelled from a Cistercian monastery for "carnal and worldly desires."

Lanz, a teacher's son, was born in Vienna in 1874. He changed his birthdate and place of origin to mislead astrologers. As a child, his wish had been to become a Knight Templar and to own Templar chateaux or, at least, to reconstruct them. His strongest impression as a youth had been an opera, *The Templar and the Jewess*, which transported him into ecstasy. (Occultists have always argued that the Templars, a medieval religious and military order, were a Gnostic sect working to purify the world of evil.) In 1893, at the age of nineteen, he entered the Cistercian monastery Holy Cross, which had an important place in Austrian history. The following year, he issued a work about a discovery which held secret meaning for him: a monument from the period of the Crusades, of a manly figure treading barefoot on an animal-like human being. In this relief sculpture Lanz saw the triumph of the higher races over the lesser races, and it became the symbol of his ideology.

In 1900, a year after he was expelled from the monastery, he surfaced again as "Baron von Liebenfels" and started his order, usurping the name and rituals from his beloved Templars. His sign was the swastika; his slogan, "Race fight until the castration knife." This studious-looking, bespectacled young man, as much the model of a minor official as his kindred soul, Himmler, preached a fall from a race-pure paradise that came about when the "Arioheroiker" interbred with the "Dark Races," or "Demonic Slopwork." The hero, Frauja (the Gothic name for Jesus), came to save the Aryan women from the original sinner of *"Sodomie"* through the commandment "Love thy neighbor as thyself—if he is a member of your own race." This Lanz took to be the teaching of the Catholic Church in the Middle Ages. He called his theory Ariosophy.

As crazy as this may sound, Lanz quickly found people who were willing to believe—and some of the believers were wealthy men, ready to help Lanz make his wildest dreams come true. With their help, he bought the castle of Werfenstein in Lower Austria, in 1907. Other castles, in Marienkamp near Ulm and on the island of Rügen in the Baltic, were also converted into temples where the order conducted elaborate Grail ceremonies. The carefully screened initiates, awesome in white hooded robes, performed celebrations written by Lanz. Using his monastic training, he also composed his own voluminous variations of liturgical texts: a two-volumed *New Templars' Breviary, The Psalms in German*, and a "secret Bible for the initiated" which ran to ten volumes, as well as prayer books and the like. The race struggle was his major concern, but the order also dabbled in astrology, the Cabala, phrenology, homeopathy, and nutrition. After reconstructing somewhat the Werfenstein castle, fitting it out with Templar symbols of ritual magic, and raising up a swastika flag, never before seen in that part of the world in modern days, he made plans for world salvation. To ensure "the extirpation of the animal-man and the propagation of the higher new man," he called for a radical program: genetic selection, sterilization, deportations to the "ape jungle," and race extermination by forced labor or murder. "Offer sacrifices to Frauja, you sons of the gods!" Lanz wrote. "Up, and sacrifice to him the children of the Schrättlinge." He advocated the establishment of special breeding colonies for the production of more Aryans.

He called his major work nothing less than *Theozoologie oder die Kunde von den Sodoms-Affligen und dem Götter-Elektron. Eine Einführung in die älteste und neueste Weltanschauung und eine Rechtfertigung des Fürstentumes und des Adels* ("Theo-zoology or the Lore of the Sodom-Apelings and the Electron of the Gods. An Introduction into the Oldest and Newest Philosophy and a Justification of Royalty and Nobility").

He believed Aryan heroes, "Masterpieces of the gods," to be possessed of splendid electromagnetic-radiological organs and transmitters which gave them special powers. By following his eugenic measures, they would revitalize their lost faculties. Joachim Fest, one of Germany's leading journalists, comments on this in his book, *Hitler*:

> The age's anxiety feelings, elitist leanings toward secret societies, fashionable idolization of science by dabblers in the sciences, all tied together by a considerable dose of intellectual and personal fraud, combined to shape this doctrine.
>
> . . . [Lanz] was one of the most eloquent spokesmen of a neurotic mood of the age and contributed a specific coloration to the brooding ideological atmosphere, so rife with fantasies, of Vienna at that time.

Exactly what had Hitler to do with Lanz? In *Mein Kampf* the only possible reference to *Ostara* may be this one: "For the first time in my life I bought myself some anti-Semitic pamphlets for a few heller." His friend from childhood, August Kubizek, mentions that during this period Hitler joined an anti-Semitic lodge. But according to Lanz's biographer, Wilfried Daim, not only was Hitler a regular reader of *Ostara*, but, because he had missed several issues, he looked up Lanz himself in 1909, who was happy to supply him with back copies. In fact, says Daim, he saw Lanz a few times and "left an impression of youth, pallor, and modesty." Fifteen months later, through three changes of residence, the copies were still in Hitler's possession. Lanz claimed him as one of his disciples, writing to an occultist in 1932: "Hitler is one of our pupils. You will one day experience that he, and through him we, will one day be victorious and develop a movement that makes the world tremble."

Hitler attempted to bury all his earlier influences and his origins, and he spent a great deal of energy hiding them. Lanz was forbidden to publish after Germany annexed Austria in 1938. Hitler ordered the murder of Reinhold Hanisch, a friend who had shared the down-and-out days in Vienna. But the influence of Lanz's Ariosophy is evident in passages like these from *Mein Kampf*:

> By defending myself against the Jew, I am fighting for the handiwork of the Lord. . . . This Jewification of our spiritual life and mammonization of our mating instinct will sooner or later destroy our entire offspring. . . .
>
> Blood sin and desecration of the race and the original sin in this world and the end of a humanity which surrenders to it.

With satanic joy in his face, the black-haired Jewish youth lurks in wait for the unsuspecting girl whom he defiles with his blood, thus stealing her from her own people. With every means he tries to destroy the racial foundations of the people he has set out to subjugate. Just as he himself systematically ruins women and girls, he does not shrink back from pulling down the blood barriers for others, even on a large scale. It was and it is the Jews who bring the Negroes into the Rhineland, always with the same secret thought and clear aim of ruining the hated white race, by the necessarily resulting bastardization, throwing it down from its cultural and political height, and himself rising to be its master.

Here, surely, is the same paranoid, sex-obsessed imagination as the renegade monk's. Though we may never have certain knowledge as to whether or not Hitler was a member of the New Templars, there is ample reason to suppose that Lanz's nasty vapors helped to poison the Third Reich.

The other Viennese occultist who attracted Lanz's disciples, Guido von List, presented a somewhat different variation of the occultist-racist package.

List was born in 1848 to a rich Viennese merchant. At fourteen, in the catacombs of St. Stefan's Cathedral in Vienna, he vowed before a dilapidated altar that when he became adult he would build a temple to the pagan god Wotan. His life's work settled, he became first a merchant and then secretary of the Austrian Alp Society. Members used the *Heil* greeting, harking back to paganism. List thought of himself as the link with an ancient race of Germanic priests and wise men called the Armanen. Their holiest emblem had been the swastika. Taking the same symbol, which had been in widespread use by many ancient peoples, he started his own secret society, the Armanen, in 1908. To the Germanic peoples, the swastika was an occult symbol for the sun, which represented life. German racists believed that one of the proofs of the inequality of races was that some had a more positive attitude toward the sun than others, and sun worship became a pagan ritual among völkisch groups. List became a pioneer in reviving Teutonic folklore and mythology. This helped to prepare the climate for nationalism.

The Armanen succeeded in attracting such people as Vienna's mayor, Karl Lueger, and the well-known Theosophist Franz Hartmann. List claimed that his group was the inner circle, hence, the leaders of the Aryo-Germanic race, with power to unlock the secrets of the universe.

They had the call. They were similar to God. They also happened to be radically anti-Semitic. List apparently never lacked for rich supporters to finance his undertakings. His major undertaking was his plan to lead the master race, which his presumed psychic powers led him to believe he was qualified to do, having been in communication with ancients possessing esoteric wisdom.

He looked like an ancient prophet with his long, flowing white beard. He taught his members runic occultism. Wotan was said to have invented the runes, the ancient alphabet, as part of his secret science. (The Gothic *runa* means "secret," "secret decision," similar to the Old Iranian *run*: "secret," "mystery." The early Finnish *runo*, taken from the Germanic, has to do with magic songs.) Edgar Polome points out in his essay "Approaches to Germanic Mythology," in *Myth in Indo-European Antiquity*: "What Odin [another name for Wotan] originally acquired by hanging on the tree for nine days, starving and thirsting as in a shamanic initiation rite, was a powerful secret lore, of which the runes later on became merely the tool."

The idea that the runes have occult significance was mentioned as early as A.D. 98 by Tacitus, who described the Germanic peoples as making marks on wood branches in order to practice augury and divination. Old Norse literature speaks of runes carved on wood, over which incantations or charms were spoken. List wrote a book about runes in 1908. Like other German occult groups, his was preoccupied with the magical power contained in the old alphabet.

List had other concerns too, according to Trevor Ravenscroft's book, *The Spear of Destiny*, largely based on the revelations of his friend Dr. Walter Stein, a Viennese scientist who was a student at Vienna University from 1909 to 1913, when Hitler was living in the city.

A deep interest in occultism, particularly the Holy Grail, led Stein to a bookshop in the old quarter of Vienna that was frequented by Hitler as well. The proprietor, Ernst Pretzsche, had a group photograph on his desk, showing himself with List, whose books on Pan-German mysticism were enjoying a great vogue. But the press had revealed black magic practices, sending Vienna into a furor. List was unmasked as the leader of a blood brotherhood which went in for sexual perversions and substituted the swastika for the cross. The Viennese were so shocked that List had to flee from Vienna. Ravenscroft reports that Dr. Stein told him how Hitler attained higher levels of consciousness by means of drugs and made a penetrating study of medieval occultism and ritual magic, discussing with

him the whole span of the political, historical and philosophical reading
through which he formulated what was later to become the Nazi
Weltanschauung.

Pretzsche had introduced Hitler to consciousness-expanding drugs, as
well as to astrological and alchemical symbolism. Hitler told Stein that
Pretzsche had been present when List tried to materialize "the Incubus" in
a ritual designed to create a "Moon Child."

Altering states of consciousness by means of drugs or sexual perversions
are not unknown to occult groups. By daring to break taboos against acts
which would disgust other people, one might gain powers of which
ordinary men did not dream. Hitler's later reputation for unnatural practices (coprophilia, masochism) may well have been deserved—may, in
fact, have been inspired by tutors such as Lanz and List.

The historian Reginald H. Phelps, although he does not touch on the
occult practices of Lanz and List, points out in his article " 'Before Hitler
Came': Thule Society and Germanen Orden," in *The Journal of Modern
History*, that they propagated their theories "with varying success among
intelligentsia and aristocrats as well as among that famous foundering petty
bourgeoisie that is supposed to be the chief consumer of such wares; the
same names run through the same arguments and blow up the same
balloons of theory, year after year, in book after book."

About 1912, disciples of Lanz and List started the Germanen Orden
under the leadership of a member of List's Armanen, a journalist named
Philipp Stauff, and several others.

Theodor Fritsch, one of the founders, had great organizational ability.
Originally a technician for windmills, he then published a trade journal for
millers, the *Deutscher Müller*, which provided him with the funds to
pursue his real passion, "scientific" anti-Semitism. Besides, windmillers
represented a dying branch of the economy. From the 1880's on he had
been a leader in the Pan-German movement. His books and tracts brought
him a certain notoriety. In 1902, he began to publish the *Hammer*, a racist
scandal sheet which aimed at eliminating all Jewish participation from
German cultural life. He tried to spread the word to the workers as well
as to the elite, calling for a racist-nationalist organization that would com-
bine the smaller groups into one "above the parties." It was to be im-
peccably Aryan and was to bring "enlightenment" to the Germanic peoples.

He was joined by a sealer of weights and measures from Magdeburg,
Hermann Pohl, and also by Stauff, who brought with him several other List

disciples. The organization was to be a secret Bund for the purpose of combatting what they believed to be the Jewish secret Bund, which was plotting world conspiracy. One could only become a member by proving German origin to the third generation. Race science was to be taught, provable in the same way for human beings as the principles of scientific breeding had been established for plants and animals. The origin of all sickness was the result of the mixing of races, they held. The principles of Pan-Germanism were to be disseminated not only among Germans but among all blood-related peoples. The fight was against all un-German thinking, which included Judaism and internationalism.

While the Germanen Orden violently opposed Freemasonry as international and Jew-ridden, it used Freemason terminology and organization. Pohl had a theory that this would guarantee secrecy. Also, Freemasonry's concept of brotherhood would help prevent dissension between members.

Their symbols were runes and swastikas, their costumes reminiscent of Wotan and paganism.

Stauff and Pohl were the only open members. Closet cultists have always enjoyed the high degree of secrecy surrounding the meetings of occult groups. Rites are rarely, if ever, committed to paper. It is as if there is a recognition that power tends to evaporate and mysteries to become cheapened with exposure. At any rate, the initiation and other rites must have been similar to those of the Freemasons and Lanz's and List's groups. As with those other groups, there were inner and outer circles, with the latter yearning to be admitted into the ranks of the former.

The mysteries were revealed through signs and symbols which only the properly initiated could interpret, and only when deemed worthy. The typical occultist saw symbolism everywhere, and hermetic significance in everything. Groups also borrowed heavily from each other, so that if one saw wisdom in the ancient rune symbols, chances were that another would adopt it. Stauff and List wrote books on runic wisdom. Meetings of the Germanen Orden taught the same.

Before World War I, despite countless leaflets distributed and propaganda spewed out, growth of the Germanen Orden was slow. Fritsch issued a call to action. The time for counterrevolution was at hand. For decades the Germanic peoples had been sabotaged by the Tschandale, Lanz's term for the lower races. Now the "chief criminals" must be defeated. "A few hundred courageous men can accomplish the work," said Fritsch. The Jewish liberal leaders

must fall, at the very start of the revolt; not even flight abroad shall

protect them. As soon as the bonds of civic order lie shattered on the
ground and law is trodden underfoot, the Sacred *Vehme* enters on its
rights; it must not fear to smite the mass-criminals with their own
weapons.

The group, however, was not successful. Pohl, despite his concern with
the binding cement of brotherhood, managed to quarrel with everyone.
The war put the finishing touches on its defeat. Pohl wrote to a member
in November 1914, Phelps reports,

that finances were bad, nearly half the brethren were with the military;
"the war came on us too early, the G.O. was not yet completely
organized and crystallized, and if the war lasts long, it will go to
pieces." The childish play of ritual and ceremony in the Orden wearied
the members. . . . Pohl seemed to think that the banquets were the chief
thing. . . .

Between 1914 and 1918 the Orden was inactive, because most of its
members were at the front.

Of the known members, only Theodor Fritsch, the "grand old man" of
German anti-Semitism, achieved lasting recognition. His *Anti-Semitical
Catechism*, written in 1887, had more than twenty editions and sold almost
a hundred thousand copies. His *Handbook of the Jewish Question*, a 1919
update of the *Catechism*, reached 145,000 readers. Some years ago, in a
suburb of Berlin, a monument was erected to his name.

During the war, all the secret cults were dormant. Pohl was reduced to
selling bronze rings inscribed with runic characters. They possessed, he
claimed, protective magical qualities, certainly very much needed in those
days.

It was not until after the war that the occult anti-Semitic groups produced
a mass movement.

CHAPTER 4

The Thule Society

> In the depths of his subconscious every German has one foot
> in "Atlantis" where he seeks a better Fatherland and a better
> patrimony.
>
> —Hermann Rauschning, *Hitler Speaks*

After the war, it was not uncommon to find occult secret societies coupling with politics of the conservative, racist sort and growing quite militant. The Germanen Orden was reactivated, and Hermann Pohl's Bavarian branch took the cover name of Thule.

Not until 1933 did the connection between Thule and the prehistory of National Socialism come to light, when a beefy adventurer published, in Munich, a book with the intriguing title *Bevor Hitler Kam* ("Before Hitler Came"). It must have enjoyed a vogue, because there was a second printing in 1934. Both editions were confiscated by the Nazis, and the author vanished—murdered, his publisher claimed. Hitler had already given a rather simple, straightforward account of his political debut in an insignificant workers' party, and he apparently did not care to have another version publicized.

The author, who called himself Baron Rudolf von Sebottendorff, had been Grand Master of a small lodge which called itself the Thule Society, and he stated right at the outset: "Thule people are the ones to whom Hitler first came."

Sebottendorff himself acknowledges his debt to "a man whom Juda [Jewdom] could not get rid of"—Theodor Fritsch—and to "three Austrians who started the fight against Juda": Guido von List, Jörg Lanz von Liebenfels, and List's disciple, Philipp Stauff. There was one other, a Baron Wittgenberg, who, Sebottendorff claimed, "chose to kill himself" in 1920 because his wife and daughter were "caught under the influence of a Jewish banker." This unfortunate man's compendiums, published in 1914 (*An Index of Jewish Titled People, An Index of Titled People and Their Connection with Jews*, and *Jews of Industry, Science, Authors and Artists*), had been snatched up by Jews, said Sebottendorff, and there were no more copies available.

Thule and the Germanen Orden joined forces right after the war. Sebottendorff prepared a brochure for the initiates coming home, and started a publication called *Runen* to bring in new members. The first three members of the reconstituted circle were Dr. George Gaubatz, a bald-headed Red Cross worker and member of the Audubon Society, who looked like Erich von Stroheim and wore a key chain across his waistcoat, from which dangled the swastika, emblem of the Thule Society; Wilhelm Rohmeder, an educator and member of a German education society; and Johannes Hering, who had already distinguished himself in Pan-German circles.

There were, apparently, attempts at gaining magical knowledge. Sebottendorff was an authority on astrology, alchemy, divining rods, and rune symbolism, happy to expatiate on these subjects. Johannes Hering's diary entry for August 17, 1918, shows great vexation with Sebottendorff for delivering a talk to the group on divining rods. Hering feared "such occult nonsense lost them good will."

Sebottendorff was nostalgic for the Middle Ages, when the Jews in Germany had been openly persecuted. Nowadays, he said, they exerted an influence not only on the Catholic Church, but, through Freemasonry, even on the Protestants. In fact, the Jews were always the "*machers*" in the Masonic lodges, and plotted an international conspiracy, under the guise of liberty, fraternity, and equality. Sebottendorff mouthed the usual attitudes of völkisch writers toward Freemasons, who have traditionally been associated with the forces of liberalism. The Pan-Germans pledged themselves to combat the "world conspiracy" being led by "Freemasons and international Jewry."

However, Sebottendorff had a love-hate relationship with the Freemasons. They were the prototype for most secret organizations. "The old Freemasonry," he said, "had been a keeper of secrets which they had learned from the Aryan wisdom and from the alchemists, and which concerned itself with the building of cathedrals.'' Naturally, he supposed, when the cathedrals were all built, the Masonic guilds had died out, and with them, the Aryan wisdom.

Like other occultists, Sebottendorff accepted the view that the medieval master builder knew more than just the secrets of his trade. Many of the European cathedrals, four hundred years in construction, exemplified, in esoteric circles, the occult symbolism. As a modern Freemason, Delmar Duane Darrah, described it in *The History and Evolution of Freemasonry*:

Everywhere was the mystic number. The Trinity was proclaimed by the nave and the aisle (multiplied sometimes to the other sacred number, seven), the three richly ornamented recesses of the portal, the three towers. The rose over the west was the Unity, the whole building was a Cross. The altar with its decorations announced the real perpetual Presence. The solemn crypt below represented the underworld, the soul of man in darkness and the shadow of death, the body awaiting the resurrection.

Even the uninitiated could feel the power of the symbolism underlying the great cathedrals.

Sebottendorff recognized that for the Mason himself, the work of building cathedrals was symbolic of and important to the soul's journey, as all work was. But, he said, "after the Thirty Years' War, Juda started Freemasonry again," with a difference. An article in the July 21, 1918, edition of *Runen* gives Sebottendorff's views on the antithesis between modern Freemasonry and the Aryan wisdom:

We look at our world as a product of the people. The Freemason looks at it as a product of conditions.

We don't acknowledge the brotherhood of people, only blood brotherhood. We want the freedom, not of herds, but of duty. We hate the propaganda of equality. Struggle is the father of all things. Equality is death. . . .

For Sebottendorff, the modern Freemason, like the Jew, was a parasite, unbending, incapable of change—ironic, considering the reputation for liberalism of the Freemason and Jew, and the conservatism of racist-nationalists. All the same, he borrowed liberally from the Freemasons, as well as from Madame Blavatsky, perhaps influenced by her boldness as much as by her Theosophy.

Sebottendorff, born with the less glamorous name of Adam Rudolf Glauer to a Silesian locomotive conductor in Hoyerswerda, on November 9, 1875, the same year that Countess Blavatsky was launching her Theosophical Society in America, became first a merchant seaman. At twenty-six, he transplanted himself to Turkey, and became a Turkish citizen. In 1909, he had the good fortune to be adopted by an Austrian baron named Heinrich von Sebottendorff, in Istanbul, according to Turkish law. Rudolf was badly wounded in the Balkan War and came back to Breslau in 1913. The adoption was contested in Germany, and in 1920 the last remaining members of the Sebottendorff family readopted him in Baden-Baden.

During his sojourn in Turkey, with his sinecure as engineer-cum-supervisor of a substantial estate, he had been able to spend time reading Oriental philosophy and Theosophical writings, as well as engaging in Sufi meditation.

He acknowledged that he had been a Knight of the Masonic Order of Constantine. Turkish Freemasonry, it seemed, had kept the ancient Aryan wisdom intact. "It must be shown," said Sebottendorff, "that Oriental Freemasonry still retains faithfully even today the ancient teachings of wisdom forgotten by modern Freemasonry, whose Constitution of 1717 was a departure from the true way."

By 1918 he had formed his own lodge, the Thule Society, and elevated himself to the rank of Grand Master.

One of his first acts was to place an advertisement in the local paper, inviting men to a meeting. Those who responded were sent a letter, predicting the imminent collapse of Germany if racial intermarriage were not halted. Each prospective member was to be on probation for one year. The initiation fee was twenty marks; the quarterly *Ardensnacht*, ten marks. The applicant was required to fill out a form declaring that, to the best of his knowledge, not a drop of Jewish or Negro blood flowed through his or his wife's veins. On returning this, he was sent a questionnaire and asked for a photograph. A most thorough questionnaire, inquiring into such intimacies as the amount of hair on various parts of the body and asking, if possible, for an imprint of the sole of the foot on a separate piece of paper. "We then tested for race purity," says Sebottendorff, "and started an inquiry." The one-year probationary period was only the first level in the member's initiation. He had to take a ritualistic vow of absolute obedience and loyalty to the Master of the lodge. "Symbolically," said Sebottendorff, "it was the return of the lost Aryan to the German *Halgedom*."

Sebottendorff did not need to invent anything. Inspired by Blavatsky's *Secret Doctrine*, he respun the age-old myth of Atlantis, calling it Thule. Like Atlantis, Thule was believed by occultists to have been the magic center of a vanished civilization. Madame Blavatsky speculated that it had been swept away in the first Deluge, 850,000 years ago. Compared with it, the much more recent Noah's Flood had been a puddle, and mythical, besides. One could get some idea of the appearance of the inhabitants of the island of Atlantis by studying the colossal statues at Easter Island. Here, Madame Blavatsky believed, were the relics of the giants of the Fourth Race; only this Atlantean being deserved to be called "MAN," for only he was completely human. After him, the Fall. Among other things, the Fall supposedly cost him his invaluable third eye, which gave him spiritual insight.

What had caused the Fall? Tucked away in *The Secret Doctrine* is the answer: The Atlanteans had mated with semi-human beings. Anticipating the argument that this was contrary to nature, she argued: "Esoteric science replies to this that it was in the very beginnings of physical man. Since then, Nature has changed her ways, and sterility is the only result of the crime of man's bestiality. . . ."

In the chaos and distress of Germany after World War I, with the occultist boom, the German racist groups seized upon mystical speculations of this sort and wove them into a myth of the master race. Sebottendorff transposed Blavatsky's complicated cosmology, by which she had sought to confound the evolutionists. In place of her sub-races who had extinguished the "Flames" by "long generations of bestiality," ruining it for the Aryans, he taught members of Thule that the purity of their blood had been defiled by the Jews. Thus, as his predecessors, List and Lanz, had done, Sebottendorff gave status to the lower and middle classes, who must have fantasized wistfully of having aristocratic blood—the only sure way to amount to something in that time and place. Not only did this mystical doctrine elevate them to potential Aryan supermen (the dormant occult powers would reawaken in the Aryan people in the twentieth century, with the appearance of "supermen" who would restore the German folk to their ancient glory and lead them in conquering the world), but it released them from the binding strictures of the Judeo-Christian morality, which had been, after all, inspired by the enemy, and calculated to rob the pagan heroes of their vitality.

With the old order going down to destruction, people felt threatened on all sides by the specter of "progress"—the frighteningly rapid growth of alien populations in the cities and the advent of mass production and modern technology—and, above all, the feeling that an imminent revolution would come to turn everything upside-down.

Sebottendorff owed a considerable part of his success to these fears. He was an accomplished astrologer and magus. His mission, as he saw it, was to reveal certain basic esoteric secrets, to counteract a vast network of alchemists and Freemasons and Jews who had hatched a plot of monstrous dimensions to undermine the civilized world. The existing religious institutions had apparently grown too weak to make any unified effort to resist. There was only one way to avoid the chaos that would throw everything into the abyss, and that was the intervention of the spiritual chiefs in the West.

The ideology of purity of the blood was founded on the esoteric alchemical theory of the Grand Work. It was necessary for Sebottendorff to prepare suitable Aryan candidates for their proper place in a mystical hierarchy. Therefore, he taught them certain mystico-magical exercises which the French occult scholar René Alleau defines as

a *Yoga* founded on the repetition of certain syllables during periods determined by the synodic revolution of the moon and in association with signs of the hand and passes that had for a goal capturing the most subtle radiations of the original force for the purpose of integrating them into the human body and to spiritualize matter into universal energy.

This is reminiscent of the conjurations and incantations which occultists have always used in the practice of the black arts. Alleau points out:

For example, to make the sign "I" one closes the right hand and extends the index finger toward the outside of the closed palm. The sign "A" is represented by the hand held so that all the fingers are situated on one plane, while the thumb forms, with the index finger, a right angle. . . .

These movements of the hand are then held at various parts of the body—neck, chest, stomach. One concentrates mentally on these gestures and the repeated syllables until, little by little, according to Alleau, an abnormal heat increases progressively and is conducted to different points in the body. At the same time, changes in the senses of taste and smell are observed, and ultimately "the disciple will see a black shadow that marks the end of the first part of the work."

When that happens, "the day is celebrated like the beginning of a new life, and the disciple receives his lodge name. . . ."

The initiate perceives colors changing, which signifies his subtle transmutation from one phase to the next. "The black of the shadow changes itself to blue, to light red, and to pale green. When the tint has become a luminous green this period is finished."

Next, in conjunction with "passes" of the chest, comes a glaring white. Alleau says:

After the "ventral posture," these mystico-magical exercises end in the elaboration of a shadow of a pomegranate red. "The Oriental Mason has become the perfect master. The cubic stone is entirely shaped." The Oriental initiates . . . name these tasks of the "spiritual Work" the "Science of the Key" and name themselves the "Sons of the Key."

That there is a colored light-field around human bodies and that the colors change with changing spiritual development is an old esoteric belief. These colors, or auras, are allegedly visible to clairvoyants and sensitives. The colors, while presumably present for these people, are also symbolic, and there are varying interpretations as to the significance of each.

All of Sebottendorff's rituals had as their aim one effect, the same as that of other esoteric groups: dissolving the "small self" so that the "divine self" could become manifest. The teaching holds that there is a world beyond the senses which can be reached with proper preparation. It is not material. The occultist believes he can ascend to it in various stages, each of which has its own particular pitfalls. It is certainly not for everyone. A great effort of will is necessary. So is courage. It is not possible to get anywhere by moving haphazardly from one stage to the next. One must observe the strictest protocol and techniques. For this, of course, the services of a master are absolutely indispensable. Demons lie in wait everywhere, and the journey is most perilous. Sebottendorff taught:

Once come to the end of our training, we sense our terrestrial body becoming more and more a stranger to us. We cross beyond it. We see

distinctly that it has become dust and ashes. It is the lowest point that can
be attained, that where the shadows of death and their terrors involve us.
It is for this reason that the ancient Oriental Freemasons received into
their community nothing but courageous men because the tests reserved
for the neophyte were very harsh. Courage and endurance were the two
principal virtues that were necessary.

To this end, Sebottendorff exacted from his disciples the cry Sieg Heil
("Glory Hail!"), which symbolizes the kind of blind obedience the Arab
formula speaks of when it exhorts the initiate: "Be between the hands of
your sheikh like a cadaver in the hands of him who washes him." The
master, in esoteric teaching, like the sheikh, is God's emissary. The
relationship between disciple and master is particularly meaningful in the
occult tradition. The neophyte must place himself completely in the
teacher's hands and obey even his most eccentric commands, whether or
not those commands do violence to his own individual conscience. There
are at least two reasons for this: First, the master is the repository of ancient
and secret wisdom which the disciple presumably cannot acquire in any
other way, and second, the master seeks deliberately to create an atmosphere in which the disciple's consciousness will be changed. Toward that
end, the master is prepared—in fact, it is necessary—to go beyond rational
thought and behavior. For this, extremely harsh discipline may be called
for.

History provides a number of examples of irrational cults by powerless
people who fell under the domination of a powerful master and accomplished his will.

The Assassins, a secret politico-religious order of eleventh-century
Islam, made the murder of its enemies a religious duty. An absolute ruler
presided over three deputy masters. Under them were the initiated, and
then the students, who were only partially acquainted with the secrets of the
order. The students in time graduated into the ranks of the initiated. Below
the students came the active members of the order, "the devoted ones,"
young men who were kept in absolute ignorance of the teaching of the sect,
but from whom complete obedience was expected. They were the blind
instruments in the work of secret political assassination planned by the
leaders. The terrorism they spread for two centuries was disproportionately
greater than their actual numbers, and the name "Assassin" became
associated with dread in the Middle East. They struck down generals,
statesmen, and caliphs. They were even hired by contending political
factions. The secret of their power lay primarily in the peculiar manner of

their training. Before they were assigned to their tasks, the disciples were stupefied by means of hashish ("Assassin" is just the English analogue of the Arabic *hashshashin*, one who is addicted to hashish), and, while in an ecstatic state, plunged into sensual pleasure, as a foretaste of the bliss which would be theirs in paradise if they faithfully followed the orders of their superlords. The training was so marvelously effective that the young men were indifferent to the threat of death, which gave them a considerable edge over their opponents.

The Thugs of India were comparable. A religious fraternity of Hindu origin, they were known to commit murders in honor of the goddess Kali as early as 1290, and lived chiefly on plunder. (Thug=conceal, hence a cheat in Sanskrit.) They were highly organized gangs traveling about India for more than three hundred years. They had a jargon and signs, and the character of their assassinations conformed to certain ancient religious rites, pointing back to the destructive power of nature. Through spies, they would learn of wealthy people undertaking a journey and strangle them with a cloth. Another class of Thugs murdered people in charge of children and then sold the children into slavery. They really formed a caste, hereditary for the most part, although a few recruits were admitted from outside. A number of Muhammadans joined. But no washermen, sweepers, musicians, poets, blacksmiths, carpenters, oil vendors, cripples, or lepers could become Thugs. After each murder, there would be a special ritual in honor of Kali, the feminine aspect of nature's demonic power.

In addition to all the other dangers, then, the disciple of an esoteric group runs the real danger of falling victim to a domination which may indeed leave him little more than a living cadaver.

Like all other such groups, Thule had an inner circle and an outer circle. Both were involved in raising their consciousness to an awareness of nonhuman intelligences in the universe and in trying to achieve means of communicating with these intelligences. Some writers have speculated that the inner circle were Satanists, who practiced black magic. Satanism is, of course, not unknown in esoteric circles. It is simply the crooked path to self-transcendence. There is even a philosophical rationale, Gnostic in origin: Since the world's ways are illusory and evil, the creation of Satan, all worldly behavior is equally sinful. The occultist, therefore, has two choices open to him. He can either become an ascetic and renounce the world or, since he recognizes the nonmateriality of the divine nature, he may feel morally free to defy convention and indulge his passions to the full.

Whether Thule members chose the "left-hand path" or not, it is certain that, like other occult groups, they aped Freemasonry. One reason why secret societies like Thule imitated the earlier prototype, despite their enmity toward it, was that it had a history of guarding ancient secrets. In a series of pamphlets published in Germany in the early seventeenth century, at a time when the upheavals of the Renaissance and Reformation had called into question many verities, this mysterious fraternity announced that it possessed spiritual knowledge of supernatural truths which could be revealed only to specially prepared initiates. It became fashionable for wise men to belong to the Freemasons, and their rituals and techniques were widely copied by other groups.

Thule gave its members a set of symbols and a place to voice their alienation. In exchange for obedience, it promised protection. In the face of the unstable economic and social conditions, the initiate received assurance that there were forces which, through magic, he could make work for him. More important and immediately satisfying, the elaborate hierarchy in which the initiate advanced only if he did as he was told meant that one could at least control other people and assert his superiority over them. Membership in Thule set one apart from nonmembers, inferior beings. The advantage that accrued to Thule members more than made up for the totalitarian aspects: Without having to make independent decisions, they could become an elite cadre whose task was nothing less than saving the world.

To deal with that task, the Thule Society became the active political branch of the Germanen Orden after the war. Without undue modesty, Sebottendorff observed of his branch: "This decision was important, for Bavaria has thereby become the cradle of the National Socialist movement."

CHAPTER 5

Riffraff into Supermen

As soon as the bonds of civic order lie shattered on the ground
and law is trodden underfoot, the *Sacred Vehme* enters on its
rights; it must not fear to smite the mass-criminals with their
own weapons.

—Theodor Fritsch

After the war, the democratic regime symbolized, to the völkisch mind,
Jewish control. The protest against economic, political, and social difficul-
ties became an "anti-Jewish revolution." Shell-shocked Germans came
home after the ordeal of the fighting and the defeat to find chaos and hunger
in the streets. They remembered the anti-Semitic propaganda they had
heard and read before the war. It was reinforced by new propaganda: The
Jew was the anarchist, the Communist, the one who had caused the defeat
and would bring down the world. In such an atmosphere of terror, the
Thule Society prospered.

It was clear to Sebottendorff that the small room on the Zweigstrasse
where the group had been meeting would no longer serve if it was to
expand. Now meetings were held every Saturday—the day of Saturn—in
the elegant Munich hotel Vier Jahreszeiten ("Four Seasons"), whose
proprietor was a member of Thule. Sebottendorff rented the rooms of a
naval officers' club and adorned them with the Society's arms—a curved
swastika pointing right, plus sword and wreath. The rooms could accom-
modate three hundred people.

"Here," said Sebottendorff, "objectives could be attained."

The consecration of the new meeting place was attended by the chairman and committee of the Germanen Orden's Berlin chapter. They officially made Sebottendorff a representative of theirs and a Master, and accepted the name Thule as a cover for the Orden. A week later, when thirty people were consecrated to the first grade, it was decided that every third Saturday of the month was to be dedicated as a consecration lodge, and on all other Saturdays, talks were to be held. The group was kept busy with meetings, initiations, and excursions at least once a week, as well as talks on such subjects as divining rods, mysticism, and bardic ritual. Every member wore a bronze pin which was designed as a shield upon which were two spears crossing a swastika.

Sebottendorff bought the newspaper *Der Münchener Beobachter* because he felt that proselytizing against the enemy could not be done as effectively through the spoken word as through the press. Though *Der Münchener Beobachter* was a sports paper, Sebottendorff was attracted to it for several reasons. The readership was young; it was impossible to start a new paper because of the paper shortage and because the government did not allow new papers to appear; and, most important, "The Jew had no interest in sports, if it did not have any monetary advantage, so the Jew would not buy and read the paper. Therefore, a sports paper could make propaganda without being detected."

Sebottendorff was wrong, of course, but showed no awareness of this, as he went on, blithely contradicting himself: "How right these calculations were is shown by the Jewish ire against the editor. They called the paper itself 'unimportant.' "

The paper had been established in 1887. The former publisher, now deceased, had been a client of the attorney Gaubatz, the Thule member; and Sebottendorff bought the publishing rights from his widow for five thousand marks. The paper had no subscribers and was distributed on the street. Sebottendorff himself was the editor. The first edition was five thousand copies.

Early issues were given over to the exhortation to "keep your blood pure" and to propaganda about the Jew as "parasitic capitalist" and participant in the black market. According to Sebottendorff: "This was something Munich never heard of. . . . In addition to the big questions, we did not forget the details. We were very critical about everything."

By November 1, 1918, the Thule organization had 1,500 members in all Bavaria, 250 of them in Munich. The paid membership journeyed to Berlin to be indoctrinated in further propaganda.

The meeting on Saturday, November 9, 1918, was a crucial one. The war was ending, the monarchy collapsing. The Jew, Kurt Eisner, had taken control of the Bavarian government two days earlier. A series of revolts had just broken out which promised chaos for the whole country. Munich, in fact, was engulfed in revolution. The old order had proven itself bankrupt, not only in Germany and Austria, but in Russia. The bolshevism which had triumphed there was the big bugbear feared by the middle and upper classes in Germany and Austria. The toppled empire in Germany created a vacuum in which revolutionaries of the right and left fought for domination. Conspirators were everywhere. German radicals looked to Russia for guidance and financial support. Munich was one of the key cities for revolutionary activity, and the little anti-Semitic lodges now consolidated into something like a mass movement.

At the November 9 meeting, Sebottendorff told the members:

Yesterday we lived through the whole breakdown of what was good and holy to us. Instead of our blood-related Kaiser, there now reigns Juda. We have to fight the Jew. . . . He who cannot follow me, despite his oath of loyalty to me—he should get out. I won't be angry about it. He who wants to stay with me, he should know that there is no going back, but only forward. He who wants to stay should remember his oath even until his death. I myself assure you and swear to you by the holy sign, listen to the victorious sun. I also will be loyal to you. Trust in me as you have trusted in me before. . . .

He then lapsed into mythological metaphysics, reminding them that their god was Walvater, the self-born power and spirit, whose rune was the Aarune (Aryan; fire; sun; eagle; sun-wheel; swastika) and whose Trinity was Wodan [Wotan], Wili, and We. Lest the members find this a bit obscure, he admonished: "Never would a low-class brain comprehend the unity of a Trinity. Wili is, like We, the polarization [of] Walvater, and Wodan the godly immanent law."

The Trinity originated, he said, from the first creation. It then created the world, and the first human pair. Wodan created the self or spirit of the life power. Wili gave the thought and the will, and We the feeling and emotions.

What did this odd mixture of ancient Eastern philosophy and Norse mythology have to do with the revolution raging outside the Vier Jahreszeiten? It provided a rationale for the dangerous mission the members were being called on to accomplish:

My friends, as of today, the red eagle is our symbol. It should point to the fact that we may have to go through death to live.

The Jews know very well that they have to fear the Aar, as it even says in the holy scriptures, fifth book of Moses, 28:49, "and the Lord will awaken unto you a people from far away, from the end of the earth, which flies like an eagle, a people whose language you do not understand."

With this pep talk, Sebottendorff cursed any member who procrastinated or compromised, who did not join in the eight o'clock consecration the following day, the birthday of Luther and Schiller. The Master adjourned the meeting with a schmaltzy poem by Philipp Stauff.

No one, of course, dared to miss the meeting on November 10—no one except Sebottendorff himself, who was laid low with a fever.

The Armistice became official the next day, and the Thule Society quietly prepared for counterrevolution. Its members could not accept the surrender of the German Army nor the proclamations of the republican government.

Conditions after the war were intolerable. Food was almost impossible to get, and jobs even scarcer. It was not uncommon to see wounded war veterans begging in the streets. With production crippled and inflation rampant, the country became a vast starvation camp. In five years' time, from 1918 to 1923, the mark had sunk to one-fifth its value, which reduced the middle class to poverty. In the harsh winter, people searched everywhere for coal and kindling. One observer remarked: "If a store offered dog biscuits a long line formed outside to procure them. People ate whatever they could find. Horsemeat became a delicacy, potato a luxury."

But for the Thule Society there was a surprising upswing. Because of governmental suspicion about the possible conspiratorial nature of organizations, many Bunds were thrown out of their meeting rooms. Landlords wanted no trouble. The innocent-appearing Thule was left alone, and with its runic obsessions was able to play host to these other Bunds, who shared a similar ideology. Sebottendorff observed:

That was good, since for the first time single groups could be in proximity to each other, because it happened very often that two or three took place at one time.

In the Thule Society everything went like a pigeon coo. Here was the National Liberal Party under Hans Dahn. Here also were the All-

Germans under editor [Julius] Lehmann, the German School Bund under Rohmeder, the Riding Fellows, the Hammerbund. . . . In short, there was not a society in Munich that somehow represented any nationalistic aim which could not be tented in the Thule Society.

All these groups were made up, for the most part, of men who had fought in the war and returned to their country stunned to find that the prewar world had been blasted away. In these secret meetings, what they fantasized was a world better able to fulfill their longings.

It was to Thule that the civil engineer Gottfried Feder first came. He was well known in Munich for an eccentric proposal for ridding the country of all its troubles. As a crankish amateur economist, he babbled about the machinations of "Jewish high finance" which undercut "German" production. His slogan became "break the shackles of finance capital," and the way to do it was by abolishing "interest slavery." He urged Thule to try to win over the workers, who were being wooed by the left.

Anton Daumenlang, whose hobby was genealogy, worked on ancestral research. Walter Nauhaus, a sculptor, was in charge of Nordic culture. The editor Julius Lehmann argued for a coup d'état and brought weapons to store in Thule rooms. One night at dinner, Sebottendorff was seized with a premonition that the premises were going to be searched. He ran quickly and hid the arms. No sooner had he done this when an investigator came.

In conjunction with plotting counterrevolution, Thule was busy fighting other occult groups, like Rudolf Steiner's Anthroposophs. Steiner had been head of Madame Blavatsky's German branch of the Theosophical Society and had broken with it over a doctrinal dispute and started his own group. Steiner, observed Sebottendorff, "wanted to become finance minister, and propagate his system of Trinity," which, presumably, was different from Thule's. Through his system, he sought to "reform Communism" rather than destroy it. The influence of this "degenerate man, this swindler and liar," was all-encompassing. He had many disciples in Munich, but was set back, said Sebottendorff, "due to the fact that there were so many suicides and sexually abused women" among them. Before the war, he had worked with "a clairvoyant, Lisbeth Seidler, in Berlin." The pair "had connections with General [Helmuth von] Moltke and they were the ones who stopped the new recruits from going into the Marne battle when they were needed. That's how the battle was lost." Sebottendorff did not miss an opportunity to attack them in his newspaper.

42 GODS AND BEASTS

The Thule itself was not without its influence. Countess Heila von
Westarp was the Society's attractive young secretary. Another aristocratic
member was Prince Gustav von Thurn und Taxis, a name prominent
throughout Europe. Robert Payne comments, in *The Life and Death of
Adolf Hitler*, that Sebottendorff "had ingratiated himself into Munich
society, large sums of money were at his disposal, and many of the most
influential people in Munich were his disciples." This powerful occult
circle included adepts, judges, lawyers, professors, leading industrialists,
surgeons, scientists, and even former members of the royal entourage of
the Wittelsbach kings. The Bavarian minister of justice, Franz Gürtner; the
police president of Munich, Ernst Pohner; and the assistant police chief,
Wilhelm Frick, were active.

It was not surprising, then, that Thule's hidden activities were held
responsible for much of the cold-blooded terrorism in that turbulent time.
In the beginning of December, Thule members planned to capture Kurt
Eisner, the Jewish minister-president of Bavaria, who had led the revolt
against the monarchy on November 7. To Thulists, Eisner, an ethereal-
looking intellectual, champion of the League of Nations, and conciliator of
the Communists, represented everything odious.

Eisner's hundred-day reign was tinged with Bohemianism. Symphony
concerts preceded political speeches. Poetry was recited from a roving
truck which toured the streets, as if, someone observed, "a picnic and not a
revolution were going on." In executive sessions, Eisner expounded on the
inner nature of politics, which he thought was as much "of an art as
painting pictures or composing string quartets."

Shortly after Eisner's assassination on February 21, police came to
investigate Thule and search for anti-Semitic flyers. Sebottendorff
threatened that if his members were not granted immunity from arrest, they
would "take a Jew, drag him through the streets, and say that he stole a
consecrated wafer. Then you will have a pogrom on your hands that will
take you out of office at the same time." When the police assured him he
was crazy, he answered: "Perhaps, but my craziness has a mouth." He
meant, presumably, that he was a man of influence, one who could not be
silenced, which must have been the case, since no one from Thule was
arrested.

The main thrust of Thule was to consolidate the anti-Semitic organiza-
tions into militant action. Toward this end, the *Nationalsozialistische
Deutsche Arbeiterpartei* (NSDAP—National Socialist German Workers'
Party) was established on January 18, 1919, in the rooms of the hotel, and
Karl Harrer, a sportswriter for the *Münchener Beobachter*, was made the

first chairman. A small proportion of Thule members were also members of the early NSDAP.

Karl Harrer apparently still hankered after the original secret discussion meetings, where one could cultivate feelings of exclusiveness. His days as chairman were numbered, and so were Thule's as an officially recognized society. The last consecration took place on March 21, 1919. The government now insisted that groups had to be incorporated, and the only leaders they would recognize had to be elected. "One had to abandon the Führer principle," Sebottendorff wistfully noted.

Thule members did continue to meet informally. After the Eisner assassination, the new minister-president of Bavaria fled northward to the city of Bamberg with his cabinet, to avoid an imminent takeover by the Communists. He issued a proclamation that "the regime of the Bavarian Free State has *not* resigned. It has transferred its seat from Munich. The regime is and will remain the *single* possessor of power in Bavaria." The Thule Society helped to set up a military group of anti-Communists, infiltrated Communist organizations, and was in touch with the legal Bavarian government in Bamberg. On April 13, Thule members participated in a debacle known as the Palm Sunday Putsch, which was intended to restore the Bamberg government to power in Munich and prevent the Communist takeover. The leader of the Putsch, Alfred von Seyffertitz, described a comic scene after the current head of Thule, Friedrich Knauf, had presented him with the gallant offer of six hundred men. When the actual event took place, only ten or twelve Thule men came, one of them a captain "in gala uniform! Patent leather riding boots, riding whip, monocle!" reported Von Seyffertitz. The Putsch which was to have driven out the Communists had the opposite effect. It opened the way for a true dictatorship of the proletariat.

Virtual anarchy reigned in Munich. The Communists seized control on April 14 and began taking hostages in reprisal for the murder of other Communists. Twelve days later, they invaded the Thule rooms, arresting the Countess von Westarp, Prince von Thurn und Taxis, a sculptor, a painter, a baron, a railroad official, and an industrial artist. Sebottendorff laid on Knauf the charge of failing to hide the membership lists.

Sebottendorff himself had journeyed to Bamberg in the hope of enlisting the help of the Free Corps, a paramilitary band of volunteers under the leadership of former army officers, supported by rich industrialists, pledged to defend the Bamberg government-in-exile. Together with rightist politicians and army officers, the Free Corps was getting ready to overthrow the Communists. Counterrevolutionaries in Munich helped by smuggling men, arms and money to the Free Corps. The men in the Free Corps, unfit for civilian life, had a personal stake in the fight. For them, the war had never ended. They were still intoxicated with it. Some had come straight out of school into the trenches, where they had learned how to be hard and how to make sacrifices. Postwar Germany was despicable to these men, and they were with the Thulists in wanting to restore the past. They were joined by students who felt superfluous in a society that was falling apart. They had nothing better to do than to kill and plunder.

Four days after seizing the seven Thule members, the Communist leader in Munich, Rudolf Egelhofer, ordered them shot. He claimed that they were counterrevolutionaries and, after all, accountable to civil law.

Thule members had, in fact, been smuggling men and information out of the city. They had become especially gifted at forging documents, assembling caches of weapons, and recruiting men for the Free Corps, whose volunteers were laying plans to defeat the left.

While twenty thousand Free Corps men marched on the city, the hostages were taken to Luitpold High School, which the Communists were using as a barracks as well as a jail. They were lined up against the courtyard wall and executed.

After the hostage murders, the Communists posted a notice that a "band of criminals . . . of the so-called upper classes" had been captured, "arch-reactionaries" who forged official documents to get confiscated goods, agents for the counterrevolution.

The executions caused an unprecedented wave of outrage among the citizenry. The anti-Semitic groups lost no opportunity to make effective propaganda, spreading rumors of fearful atrocities. The civil strife, which had begun right after the war, came to a horrifying climax over these murders.

Three Jews in the Communist government—Eugen Leviné-Nissen, Tobias Axelrod, and Max Levien—were alleged responsible for the deaths, as an act of vengeance against their anti-Semitic enemies, a charge which was never proved. The Free Corps, inflamed by the hostage murders, stormed through Munich, setting fire to a beer hall and fighting with mortars and hand grenades. One Free Corps unit marched through the streets singing its marching song:

> "Swastika on helmet,
> Colors black-white-red. . . ."

Soon, they would call themselves Storm Troopers.

During the civil war which followed, the Communists were defeated and the racist-nationalists received a great boost. It was, in every way, a rehearsal and a preparation for the brutalities to come later.

As to the Thule Society, it seems to have come to an end along with the seven hostages. Two days after their interment, there was a memorial service at the Thule rooms. The pulpit was draped with a captured Communist flag, but instead of the hammer and sickle, there was a swastika. The murder of the members had opened new possibilities.

Sebottendorff disappeared from Munich. He eventually returned to Istanbul, and then made his way to Mexico. He reappeared in Munich in 1933, hoping to revive Thule, but by that time the NSDAP he had helped to launch was doing very well without him. Some of the other Thule members were now in a position to implement what they had learned at those meetings on Saturdays at the Vier Jahreszeiten.

Eventually, the NSDAP assumed the power to come near to destroying Europe. That power, René Alleau observed, derived from one source:

. . . a fanatical autohypnosis which convinced disciples, succumbing to the totalitarian discipline in the promise of reaching a transcendent reality, that they were the new men the age was waiting for, that they were endowed with a secret energy which would enable them to take over Germany and the world. If they were properly prepared, mysteries would be revealed to them which would give them Satanic powers.

Incredible as it may seem, the members and guests of the Thule Society thought of themselves as potential masters of the earth, protected against all dangers. Their reign would last for a thousand years, until the next Deluge. Some of them became key figures in the Nazi party: Max Ammann, business manager of the party's newspaper and publishing house; Dietrich Eckart, who introduced Hitler to Munich society; Hans Frank, governor general of Poland; Anton Drexler, first chairman of the German Workers' party; Gottfried Feder, economic adviser; Karl Harrer, first chairman of the NSDAP; Rudolf Hess, Hitler's secretary and first adjutant; Adolf Hitler; Dr. Heinz Kurz, SS leader; Friedrich Krohn, dentist who designed Nazi swastika insignia; Ernst Röhm, leader of Storm Troopers; Alfred Rosenberg, commissioner for Eastern Affairs; Julius Streicher, *Gauleiter* (party district-leader) of Franconia.

The philosophy behind this cult, never mentioned at the Nuremberg Trials, sheds new light on the atrocities which were about to come, on the tacit sanction of them by the German people, and on the Messiah who led them.

CHAPTER 6

The Savage Messiah

The driving force behind black magic is hunger for power. . . . the black magician's ambition is to wield supreme
power over the entire universe, to make himself a god.

—Richard Cavendish, *The Black Arts*

Sebottendorff's *Führerprinzip* is basic to esoteric cults. The disciple
must blindly obey his master, who not only has secret knowledge, hidden
from the initiate, but who must create favorable conditions in which his
pupil can undergo a drastic change. This allows for actions which violate
individual conscience.

Of course, the principle of blind obedience operates outside occult
groups as well. The tendency is often seen in everyday institutions:
military, governmental, corporate. Soldiers of every army have it drilled
into them never to refuse an order. Mylai is one of the results. And this
follow-the-leader syndrome certainly played a part in Watergate. Stanley
Milgram's experiments in obedience to authority among university students demonstrated the alarming willingness of the average person to
perpetrate harmful actions on fellow human beings when he fails to
question the directives of a superior.

It is easy to see how the *Führerprinzip* led, step by step, to the surrender
of the will of the people to the will of the Führer, culminating in such
confessions as that of Rudolf Hoess, commandant of Auschwitz, just

before his execution in 1947, that he would have gassed and burned his own wife and children, and himself as well, if the Führer had asked it.

A German did not need to be an occultist in order to long for a Messiah to save him. As in other difficult periods in history, after World War I the Messiah's coming was believed to be imminent. A father-figure in a chaotic age, he would surely preserve and protect and make things bloom again in the desert where men were daily losing their bearings. Still, the poet Heinrich Heine's "man whom the German people await, the man who will bring to them the life and happiness they have so long hoped for in their dreams," was awaited with particular zeal by the members of the Thule Society. According to Trevor Ravenscroft's confidant, Dr. Stein, Thule member

> Dietrich Eckart and a small inner core of Thulists had been prepared for the imminent appearance of the German Messiah in a whole series of spiritualistic séances. . . .
> . . . all those present were terrified. . . .

Prince von Thurn und Taxis had prophesied the coming of a German Messiah, and Countess von Westarp had said that a false prophet would lead the Germans to defeat. Sebottendorff ran from the room in terror, but Eckart tackled him and knocked him down.

Eckart shared with Hitler a fascination with *Ostara*'s erotic racism; had, in fact, been charged with plagiarism by Lanz von Liebenfels himself. After the Nazis were swept into power, Lanz was to write that his Order of New Templars was "the first manifestation of the Movement which now, in accordance with the law of God, is most powerful in history and unrestrainedly sweeping over the world." Eckart already belonged to the Thule Society when Hitler appeared on the scene. It was Eckart who first promoted Hitler as the long-awaited Messiah.

What do we know of Hitler's life before then? With certain important exceptions, only what he wanted us to know: that he was the son of a harsh man, a civil servant, who wanted his son to follow in his footsteps; that he adored his mother, who died a lingering death of cancer while he was struggling in Vienna; that he did not make it as an artist; that knowledge of his true vocation came to him in World War I.

But we can paint a fuller picture than this—one that rather complicates the popular image of Hitler as a practical realist, though he most certainly was a man who knew how to seize his opportunities. He was also an occultist.

The Library of Congress in Washington contains thousands of books taken from Hitler's personal library after the Allied occupation of Germany. One of them, *Nationalismus*, is by the Indian mystic Rabindranath Tagore. It bears an inscription dated April 20, 1921, signed by the unfamiliar name B. Steininger: *"An Adolf Hitler, meinem lieben Armanenbruder"* ("To Adolf Hitler, my dear Armanen-brother").

The Armanen, Guido von List's esoteric brotherhood, invented an ancient race of Germanic priests. Their wisdom was passed on through the centuries, not only through a secret brotherhood of initiates but also through clues which List, the last of the Armanen, was able to divine through intuition and clairvoyance. Sacred meanings were hidden away in words and signs. This, of course, is perfectly understandable to the occultist. But List apparently reached a wider audience by pioneering in the revival of pagan worship.

His theories were studied by the Germanen Orden and, later, by the SS. His books, confiscated by the Allies, bear the SS mark and are stamped *Ahnenerbe*, the Nazi Ancestral Research branch, and apparently were used in teaching candidates for the SS.

But apart from the inscription to Hitler, the only connecting link from him to List is made by Ravenscroft, who reports that Hitler's occult adviser, the Viennese bookseller Ernst Pretzsche, was associated with List.

Hitler's library also contained one of Lanz's books, *Das Büch der Psalmen Teutsch: Das Gebetbuch der Ariosophen Rassenmystiker und Antisemiten* ("The Book the Psalms Teach: The Prayerbook of Ariosophic Race Mystery and Anti-Semitism").

Both List and Lanz were obsessed with blood purity, with anti-Semitism, with the secret significance of the Grail legend, with bringing about a new order. Both took the swastika for their symbol.

Membership in cults of this type are usually kept secret, so it is not surprising that we have no documentation of Hitler's membership. He may well have been a member of either the Armanen or the Order of New Templars, or both, however, for it is entirely in keeping with his character as presented by people who knew him in his younger days in Vienna.

Josef Greiner, the former lamplighter, who published his reminiscences in 1947, describes Hitler as an explorer of occult mysteries and a student of telepathy—knowledgeable about the rituals of the yogis and about fakirs who seem to control their heartbeats. He was intrigued, according to Greiner, by pseudosciences which appeal to the poorly educated.

Reinhold Hanisch, who knew both Hitler and Greiner in this period, credited Greiner with leading Hitler into the occult but it may very well have been the other way around.

Hitler had already expressed many of these ideas as a teen-ager to his young friend August Kubizek, in Linz. He had had visions of remodeling the whole town, and spent hours telling his plans to his patient friend. Kubizek complied with all his dreams:

We would go to St. Georgen on the Güsen to find out what relics of that famous battle in the Peasants' War still remained. When we were unsuccessful Adolf had a strange idea. He was convinced that the people who lived there would have some faint memory of that great battle. The following day he went again alone, after a vain attempt to get my father to give me the day off. He spent two days and two nights there, but I don't remember with what result.

The circle in which Hitler moved in Linz subscribed to the ideas of Georg von Schoenerer, an admirer of List. Hitler was more at home in German mythology than in his real world. Kubizek says: "From the *Edda*, a book that was sacred for him, he knew Iceland, the rugged island of the North, where the elements which formed the world meet now, as they did in the days of Creation. . . ."

Kubizek and Greiner both testify that what especially intrigued Hitler was the power of the human will.

The Allies, apparently puzzled by the riddle of Adolf Hitler, a ne'er-do-well of humble origins, unprepossessing looks, and mediocre intellect, rising to such eminence, had secret psychiatric reports drawn up on him while the war was still in progress, which obviously did not help much to clear away the confusion about this complex personality. They paint a portrait of sexual deviation, of adolescent overcompensation, of an indomitable will to power. This will to power has not been given its proper due. His admirers, and even reluctant observers, have testified to his spellbinding, hypnotic effect. A romantic mystic, a visionary, a charismatic figure he is often acknowledged to be. But this early will to power betrays the interests of a potential occultist.

The occultist is concerned with transcending everyday reality. He makes use of myth, symbol, and ritual. He tries to put himself in touch with forces which he believes to be beyond the reach of sense, and to awaken higher powers in himself. The Work, the *Grand* Work, is to transform oneself from an ordinary mortal into a superman. For this, the will must be developed—something the ordinary mortal neither knows nor cares about.

Hitler, from the time he was a young boy, was preoccupied with the matter of will, a concern not shared by his family or social milieu. Though he could not will himself into art school or good health, his childhood friend Kubizek was the recipient of confidences about his inner life which betray Wagnerian fantasies of another sort of strength.

After a performance of Wagner's opera *Rienzi*, both boys stood under the stars, and, says Kubizek:

I was struck by something strange, which I had never noticed before, even when he had talked to me in moments of the greatest excitement. It was as if another being spoke out of his body, and moved him as much as it did me. It wasn't at all a case of a speaker being carried away by his own words. On the contrary: I rather felt as though he himself listened with astonishment and emotion to what burst forth from him with elementary force. I will not attempt to interpret this phenomenon, but it was a state of complete ecstasy and rapture, in which he transferred the character of *Rienzi*, without even mentioning him as a model or example, with visionary power to the plane of his own ambitions. But it was more than a cheap adaptation. Indeed, the impact of the opera was rather a sheer external impulse which compelled him to speak. Like flood waters breaking their dykes, his words burst forth from him. He conjured up in grandiose, inspiring pictures his own future and that of his people.

Hitherto I had been convinced that my friend wanted to become an artist, a painter, or perhaps an architect. Now this was no longer the case. Now he aspired to something higher, which I could not yet fully grasp. It rather surprised me, as I thought that the vocation of the artist was for him the highest, most desirable goal. But now he was talking of a *mandate* which, one day, he would receive from the people, to lead them out of servitude to the heights of freedom.

It was an unknown youth who spoke to me in that strange hour. He spoke of a special mission which one day would be entrusted to him. . . .

Hitler later recalled the incident, too, and solemnly said: "In that hour it began."

Typical adolescent dreams? A flight from harsh reality? Of course. But his grandiose plans for the future, unlikely as they were, did come to pass after all, and it is plausible that he should have worked on himself systematically, in obedience to occult teaching. The occult tradition, as Madame Blavatsky pointed out, holds that what moves the world is "that mysterious and divine power latent in the will of every man, and which, if not called to life, quickened and developed by Yogi-training, remains dormant in 999,999 men out of a million, and gets atrophied."

From the ancients to the most simplistic modern exponents of the magic power of thought, the doctrine is that one's attention and intense concentration can accomplish any desired end. If the end is not reached, it is simply because the mind has not sufficiently projected it.

In Vienna, Hitler's political thinking had been influenced by Mayor Karl Lueger, who, according to the Anthroposophist, Johannes Tautz, came to the Armanen. Lueger was in office from 1897 to 1910, and, in league with the Pan-German anti-Semitic groups, found favor with the lower middle class by attacking liberals and Jews. His anti-intellectualism was epitomized by one of his underlings, who said, "When I see a book I want to puke." While List wrote pseudo-erudite tracts on the esoteric meaning of words, Lueger knew that to gain power he had to win over the largest possible segment of society.

Hitler was a peculiar fellow to his World War I buddies because he would sit listlessly by himself and let nobody stir him out of his concentration. He was apt to jump up abruptly and move around agitatedly, predicting that the Germans would be defeated. Recovering in the hospital from a gassing attack which left him temporarily blinded, he had a vision which must have been comforting, considering his dim prospects for the future. Writing of this experience in *Mein Kampf*, he said: "I resolved that I would take up political work."

When he was discharged, he continued to work for the army, in the Munich branch, as an instructor in the Press and News Bureau of the Political Department. In the course of his duties he was sent to investigate one of the satellites of the Thule Society, the German Workers' party, and ended by joining it.

His membership number in the German Workers' party was originally 555, but for some reason it was changed to 7. The discrepancy is mentioned in a footnote to Reginald H. Phelps's monograph in the *American Historical Review*, July 1963:

Drexler, outraged by distorted official radio "history" of the party's origin, drafted a long, angry letter to Hitler late in January 1940. . . . In it he stated: "No one knows better than you yourself, my *Führer*, that you were never the seventh member of the party, but at most the seventh member of the committee, which I asked you join as propaganda chief." In this letter—never sent, since Drexler planned to forward it to Hitler after the war—are also statements about the size of the party in September 1919 and about the "forging" of Hitler's party card.

It is significant that someone, at some point, saw fit to change the number. Seven, in occult terms, is a much more important number than 555. List, for instance, expatiates on seven:

> The seven is developed from a triangle. . . . it is the secret of the beginning, the development and the change into the All in all respects . . . and so closes the circle of eternity. That is why all figures in geometry can be measured by the triangle and the square. The seven is a glyphe (secret word and secret connotation) as well as a numerical value, because it can be arrived at only by symbols of the triangle and the square.

This, incidentally, is a fairly typical, if not lucid, exposition. To the occultists, numbers have curious properties which are not just utilitarian. They all borrow from Pythagoras, who first gave mathematics a specialized meaning. The occult properties of numbers form the basis for serious study which, they believe, contains the key to laws of human and cosmic life.

Whether through superstition or cognizance of cosmic laws, seven became Hitler's number. The perfect number, in short, for the membership card of the future Messiah of Germany.

But how is it that such an unexceptional fellow became the Messiah? Was he chosen by the group or by a single member—perhaps Eckart—or did he create the role for himself? This is still an open question.

According to Kurt Ludecke, who knew both Hitler and Eckart in those early years, Eckart "was something of a genius, and to a great degree the spiritual father of Hitler and grandfather of the Nazi movement. Also, he was well-to-do, one of Hitler's first financial blessings."

It is more likely that Eckart himself was not well-to-do but well-connected. He had contact with rich members of Munich's social circle and was an accomplished fundraiser. At any rate, it was he who afforded Hitler the entrée into that circle, with the grandiloquent announcement that here, at last, was the "long-promised savior." In fact, he is reported to have said to Alfred Rosenberg, after Thule's revolutionary activities: "Let it happen as it will and must, but I believe in Hitler; above him there hovers a star."

Why Eckart believed particularly in Hitler remains something of a mystery. He apparently did have an uncanny knack for persuasive speechifying. His young friend Kubizek testified to that. This talent initially focused the attention of the group on Hitler. Its effect is admirably summed up by Joseph Goebbels, who wrote to Hitler after hearing him speak in Munich in June 1922:

> Like a rising star you appeared before our wondering eyes, you performed miracles to clear our minds and, in a world of skepticism and desperation, gave us faith. You towered above the masses, full of faith and certain of the future, and possessed by the will to free those masses with your unlimited love for all those who believe in the new Reich. For the first time we saw with shining eyes a man who tore off the mask from the faces distorted by greed, the faces of mediocre parliamentary busybodies. . . .
>
> . . . You expressed more than your own pain. . . . You named the need of a whole generation, searching in confused longing for men and task. What you said is the catechism of the new political belief, born out of the despair of a collapsing, Godless world. . . . One day, Germany will thank you. . . .

Whatever others thought of him, Hitler himself was not so ambitious as to proclaim himself the Messiah right from the outset. At first, he was just a drummer, bringing glad tidings of the coming of the new man. The metaphor changed after the Putsch of 1923.

When the government was inactive in the face of Communist uprisings, Hitler and his Storm Troopers, on the evening of November 8, planned a coup to depose them. The government met that night in one of Munich's many beer halls, and the Nazis surrounded the building. On a signal, they entered the hall and fired a shot at the ceiling, shouting that the national revolution had come and the government was deposed. The Putsch turned out to be a fiasco, and when it was over, Hitler was imprisoned at Landsberg.

One of the major defendants at the Nuremberg Trials, Baldur von Schirach, the leader of the Hitler Youth, dated the change in Hitler's self-image from a later period, in talking to the prison psychiatrist after the war: "Before 1934 he was *menschlich* [human]; from 1934 to 1938 he was *ubermenschlich* [superhuman]; from 1938 on he was *unmenschlich* [inhuman] and a tyrant."

But the consensus does not seem to be that Hitler's confinement, and particularly, according to some commentators, his intimate exposure to Rudolf Hess in prison, occasioned the change. Whatever the relationship between the two men may have been, Hitler did become something of a national idol by the very fact of his imprisonment. He, of course, enjoyed the legend which began to grow up around him, and capitalized on it in every way that he could. It is not uncommon, either, for breakthroughs to come to men as they meditate quietly in prison. He certainly had lots of time to think in the nine months he was in Landsberg. It was only after this, according to his intimate acquaintance, "Putzi" Hanfstaengl, that the Führer cult began in earnest. Before then, he was *Herr Hitler* to everyone. At Hess's instigation, this now changed, first to *der Chef* and then to *Mein Führer*. Hitler seemed to enjoy the transmutation.

In prison, he had written *Mein Kampf*, with the help of Hess. When it was published, his absolute authority over the National Socialist German Workers' party was established. Whereas before, Kurt Ludecke observes, "people said he would be destroyed for loyalty to friends," he was now no longer one of the boys, but increasingly dictatorial and self-serving. From here on, Hitler, whatever steps he took, continued to see himself as sent by Providence to save the German people. This message communicated itself with striking power to his subalterns, to the masses, and even to his enemies.

Hermann Rauschning, who eventually defected from the Party, reports a typical conversation in which Hitler told Bernhard Forster, Nietzsche's brother-in-law, that he

would not reveal his unique mission until later. He permitted glimpses of it only to a few. When the time came, however, Hitler would bring the world a new religion. . . . The blessed consciousness of eternal life in union with the great universal life, and in membership of an immortal people—that was the message he would impart to the world when the time came. Hitler would be the first to achieve what Christianity was meant to have been, a joyous message that liberated men from the things that burdened their life. We should no longer have any fear of death, and should lose the fear of a so-called bad conscience. Hitler would restore men to the self-confident divinity with which nature had endowed them. They would be able to trust their instincts, would no longer be citizens of two worlds, but would be rooted in the single, eternal life of this world.

While Rauschning took these ideas as mere reflections of irrationality, they mean something else to the student of occultism. Hitler's new religion was the same brand that Lanz and List had preached: a mixture of paganism, Gnosticism, and magic. Its true purpose could only be revealed to the initiated, and only at the proper time, because only they would really grasp its import, and only when the way had been prepared. The time, of course, had also to be auspicious in an astrological sense. And the initiated, whose consciousness presumably was sufficiently expanded, would be in a position to help usher in the new religion.

Many people have testified to Hitler's medium-like powers. Much has been made of the fact that he was born in Braunau am Inn in Austria, a town which happens to have produced a disproportionately great number of people who went on to gain reputations as mediums, the most notable being Rudi and Willy Schneider. Occultists are pleased to point out that Hitler had shared with the psychic Schneider brothers their wet nurse.

But even commentators who are not receptive to occult beliefs have drawn attention to Hitler's occasional lapses into trancelike states.

Ernst Hanfstaengl recalls "his almost medium-like performances on a speaker's platform."

Hermann Rauschning repeats what Bernhard Forster had told him about Hitler:

God, or whatever we preferred to call it, life or the universal spirit, spoke to him in solitude. He drew his great power from intercourse with the eternal divine nature. . . . Added Forster. . . . "I hear those voices of which Hitler speaks. Then I feel strong, and know that we shall conquer and live for ever."

Stephen H. Roberts, an Australian journalist covering Germany in the thirties, described the two most popular views of him—either "as a mere ranting stump-orator, or as a victim of demoniacal possession, driven hither and thither by some occult force that makes him a power of evil. . . . the view of his believers that he is a demigod, revealing the path that Germany is to follow by some divine power of [intuitively] knowing what to do."

Hitler parodied Jesus. Lanz had preached that "love thy neighbor as thyself" really meant "love thy racially similar neighbor as thyself." Hitler said: "Whoever proclaims his allegience to *me* is by this very proclamation and by the manner in which it is made, one of the chosen."

Symbols of his Messiahship appeared everywhere. One of the fashionable art shops in Berlin displayed an impressive portrait of Hitler in a prominent window space, flanked with duplicates of a painting of Christ. At one of the Nuremberg rallies a giant photo of Hitler was captioned with a phrase which opens the Gospel of John—believed, by Biblical scholars, to be a Gnostic text—and which occultists are fond of quoting: "In the beginning was the Word." Sermons were preached in churches which must have caused *some* people, at least, a good deal of dis-ease, as, for example, this one: "Adolf Hitler is the voice of Jesus Christ, who desired to become flesh and blood of the German people and did become flesh and blood."

A message bearing the title "What the Christian Does Not Know About Christianity" made this astonishing point:

> If Jehovah has lost all meaning for us Germans, the same must be said of Jesus Christ, his son. He does not possess those moral qualities which the Church claims for him. He certainly lacks those characteristics which he would require to be a true German. Indeed, he is as disappointing, if we read the record carefully, as is his father.

In day nurseries, children were taught to pray:

> "Führer, my Führer, by God given to me,
> Defend and protect me as long as may be.
> Thou'st Germany rescued from her deepest need;
> I render thee thanks who dost daily me feed.
> Stay by me forever, or desperate my plight.
> Führer, my Führer, my faith, my light,
> Hail, my Führer!"

All of which lent support to Hitler's epigram in one of his more lucid moments: "What luck for the rulers that men do not think."

The Christ image was not the only one which Hitler adopted. He also had a particular fondness for Grail symbols. He put the question to Rauschning: "Should we create an elite of initiates? An order? A religious brotherhood of Templars to guard the Holy Grail, the august vessel containing the pure blood?" The quest for the Holy Grail is another of those talismans for the occultists, and Lanz and List, of course, had helped to kindle an interest in the real meaning of the Grail legend. The Grail, to the occultist, is a symbol for hidden knowledge. According to Ravenscroft, Hitler told Dr. Stein that he visualized the Grail "as a path leading from unthinking dullness, through doubt, to spiritual awakening," and that there were "ascending grades on the way to the achievement of higher levels of consciousness, disclosing the meaning of the heraldry and armorial insignia of the Knights, which he interpreted as representing the various stages they had attained in the quest for the Grail.''

He went through an elaborate explanation of the various creatures which symbolized the different degrees, the highest being the eagle, emblem of the initiate who had attained the highest powers and faculties of which man was capable, and was at last in a position to "assume a world-historic destiny." Hitler went on to say: "The real virtues of the Grail were common to all the best Aryan peoples. Christianity only added the seeds of decadence such as forgiveness, self-abnegation, weakness, false humility, and the very denial of the evolutionary laws of survival of the fittest, the most courageous and talented."

No one could accuse Hitler of false humility. Stephen H. Roberts, the Australian journalist, describes colored pictures which he saw displayed in Munich for a short time in the autumn of 1936: "of Hitler in the actual silver garments of the Knight of the Grail." Roberts believes they were withdrawn from circulation because "they gave the show away . . . were too near the truth of Hitler's mentality."

By then, Hitler's view of the Jew as the enemy of the light had bedazzled the whole country. It was the Jew who had to be cleared out of the way before the new man could arise. Lanz had proposed extermination as the most expedient way to do it. Sebottendorff, in the March 10, 1920, issue of the *Beobachter*, had been more ambiguous. He proposed, as an *Endziel* ("final goal"): *MACHT GANZE ARBEIT MIT DEM JUDEN!* ("CLEAN OUT THE JEWS ONCE AND FOR ALL!") by resorting to the "most ruthless measures, among them concentration camps" (*Sammellager*) and "sweeping out the Jewish vermin with an iron broom."

Like his teachers, Hitler saw the Jew as the embodiment of all evil, but among the qualities he considered evil were virtues such as intellect, conscience, intelligence, and pursuit of absolute truth. As he told Rauschning:

We are now at the end of the Age of Reason. The intellect has grown autocratic, and has become a disease of life. . . .

Conscience is a Jewish invention. It is a blemish, like circumcision.

A new age of Magic interpretation of the world is coming, of interpretation in terms of the Will and not the intelligence.

There is no such thing as truth, either in the moral or in the scientific sense. The new man would be the antithesis of the Jew.

The new man, Hitler told Rauschning, would be a mutation, a different biological species altogether from *homo sapiens* as we know him. This, Hitler believed, was the real seductive power of nazism. So fierce and terrible would the new men be that ordinary humans would hardly be able to look them in the face; they would be the true aristocracy, and all others would be subjects. With the coming of the new man, the inequality that exists in human life would be heightened. This was Hitler's antidote to democracy: the restoration of insurmountable barriers between two breeds of people, as he presumed to have existed in ancient great civilizations. Only Germans would have rights. Hitler had come to free them from "the dirty and degrading chimera called conscience and morality, and from the demands of a freedom and personal independence which only a very few can bear." They would be beyond good and evil. He would liberate them from "the burden of free will." He opposed "with icy clarity" the significance "of the individual soul and of personal responsibility." Judging from Hitler's popularity, the suffering masses apparently found relief in this message.

Here, again, the voice of the occultist may be heard. Since Darwin, esoteric groups have talked in terms of a mutation, though generally none but Satanists have perceived the new man as amoral.

To betray the Führer, then, was also to betray the new civilization which he was ushering in, and he managed to convince the people of this. Over and over again, in mass rallies so carefully staged that they left no one immune, he pummeled home, with the force of a master magician such as has not been seen before or since, the startling doctrine that he and the people were one. Through torchlit night parades, striking military bands, cathedral-like arcs of light, and the patterns and colors of swastika flags, a religious fervor was created among audiences wearied with waiting for hours until he came before them, suddenly, late at night, thundered his oration, and left just as suddenly. So skilled a psychologist was he that he knew that if he invited alienated mass man to "step out of his workshop," his smallness would disappear in the midst of a body of hordes "with a like conviction."

It worked. For a time, the Aryan Germans were rid of anxiety, and Hitler's mutations dared to commit unimaginable crimes against humanity, in the name of a greater humanity.

CHAPTER 7

Tibetan Wisdom Meets German Folly

Our meeting had hardly begun when my Storm Troopers—as
they became from that day forth—attacked. Like wolves they
flung themselves upon the enemy in packs of eight and ten.
How many of these men I never really knew until that day.
And at their head was gallant Rudolf, my personal secretary,
Hess.

—Hitler, *Mein Kampf*

Rudolf Hess has been painted by historians as weak and indecisive, characterless, passive, putty in the hands of a stronger man, eager to be rid of his personal identity, to give up his freedom to think and feel for himself to a totalitarian cause—in short, the perfect disciple loyal and obedient to the death. As Hitler's deputy, he must have enjoyed his dependency on the Führer.

Like Hitler, Hess had a penchant for occultism, having been steeped in it from his birth in Egypt. Born on April 26, 1896, to a prosperous Bavarian wholesaler and exporter who had transplanted himself to Alexandria, Rudolf lived with his family until his fourteenth year and then was sent to school in Germany.

As soon as World War I started, he volunteered, and was placed in the

1st Company of the 16th Bavarian Reserve Infantry Regiment, named the List Regiment, after its original commander. He was an officer in the same regiment as Hitler, who was a dispatch runner, but they never met then.

The List Regiment was in the thick of the fighting at the front. According to a letter which Hitler wrote to his old Munich landlord, they lost 2,900 men in four days. Hess was wounded twice.

When the war ended, Hess was twenty-two. He went back to Munich and joined the Thule Society. He was one of the hundreds of veterans smuggled out of Munich by Sebottendorff, along with money and arms, to join the Free Corps. Despite his hangdog look, he had a reputation for being a scrappy street fighter. He participated wholeheartedly with the Free Corps in ridding Munich of the leftist revolutionaries.

Hess was in the audience when Hitler came to German Workers' party meetings to deliver his grandiose plans for the future of the movement, predicting that the day would come "when the banner of our movement will fly over the Reichstag, over the Castle in Berlin, yes, over every German house."

Seeing the small audience and the pale, gesticulating speaker, Hess wondered, as he later reported, Was this thundering orator foolish or was he the Messiah? Soon, his mind was made up.

As a student at the University of Munich, he was eligible to apply for a prize which a wealthy South American had endowed. Competitors were to write a theme that posed the question "How Must the Man Be Constituted Who Will Lead Germany Back to Her Old Heights?"

Delirious with the Messianic hope of the time, Hess won. Drawing a word portrait of Hitler, he wrote:

> Profound knowledge in all areas of political life and history, the capacity to draw the right lessons from this knowledge, belief in the purity of his own cause and in ultimate victory, and enormous power of will give him the power of thrilling oratory which evokes joyful enthusiasm from the masses. Where the salvation of the nation is in question, he does not disdain utilizing the weapons of the adversary, demagogy, slogans, processions, etc. Where all authority has vanished, only a man of the people can establish authority. This was shown in the case of Mussolini. The deeper the dictator was originally rooted in the broad masses, the better he understands how to treat them psychologically, the less the workers will distrust him, the more supporters he will

win among these most energetic ranks of the people. He himself has nothing in common with the masses; he is all personality, like every great man.

If necessity commands it, he does not shrink from shedding blood. Great questions are always decided by blood and iron. And the question at stake is: Shall we rise or be destroyed?

Parliament may go babbling, or not—the man acts. It transpires that despite his many speeches, he knows how to keep silent. Perhaps his own supporters are the most keenly disappointed. . . . In order to reach his goal, he is prepared to trample on his closest friends. . . . For the sake of the great ultimate goal, he must even be willing temporarily to appear a traitor against the nation in the eyes of the majority. The lawgiver proceeds with terrible hardness. . . . He knows the people and their influential individuals. As the need arises, he can trample them with the boots of a grenadier, or with cautious and sensitive fingers spin threads reaching as far as the Pacific Ocean. . . . In either case, the treaties of enslavement will fall. One day we shall have our new, Greater Germany, embracing all those who are of German blood. . . .

Thus we have the portrait of the dictator: keen of mind, clear and true, passionate and then again controlled, cold and bold, scrupulous in decision, fearless in rapid execution of his acts, ruthless toward himself and others, mercilessly hard and then again soft in his love for his people, tireless in work, with a steel fist in a velvet glove, capable ultimately of overcoming even himself.

We still do not know when he will intervene to save us—this "man." But millions feel that he is coming.

By November 8, 1923, "this man" had made his presence known to all Germany. Hitler had already seized control of the Nazi party and now planned to seize control of the Bavarian government as well. Hess, intoxicated with his newly discovered Messiah, marched along with Hitler in the Munich Beer Hall Putsch of 1923. Despite its dramatic effect, the Putsch was a fiasco. When police opened fire on the marching Storm Troopers, Hitler was the first to flee. He did not mention this in *Mein Kampf*, but said of the meeting: "my Storm Troopers—as they became from that day forth—attacked. Like wolves they flung themselves upon the enemy in packs of eight and ten. How many of these men I never really knew until that day. And at their head was gallant Rudolf, my personal secretary, Hess."

Hess escaped across the border into Austria over a mountain pass. Hitler was imprisoned at Landsberg, a town just west of Munich. The punishment was very mild, lasting less than nine months, and Hitler spoke of it afterward as a much-needed vacation.

Hess proved his devotion to Hitler by coming back from Austria, giving himself up, and joining Hitler in prison, in room No. 7. So steadfast was that devotion, in fact, that Ernst Hanfstaengl hints at an unnatural relationship: "It is probably not true to say there was a physical homosexual relationship between the two, but in a passive way the attraction was there. I certainly did not trust the manhood of either. . . ."

Shared prison life served to bind the two men together until a later fiasco severed the bond. Hess became Hitler's secretary and helped him with *Mein Kampf*. Hess did more than take dictation and type the manuscript. As the best educated of Hitler's disciples, he was able to provide Hitler with useful information, particularly on a new study which was called geopolitics. He introduced Hitler to the professor (and ex-general) from whom he had learned about geopolitics, and, in fact, the professor was a frequent visitor to Landsberg prison. Some people, indeed, believe that the professor, Karl Haushofer, was Hitler's guiding brain.

Writing in *Current History and Forum* in June 1941, Frederic Sondern, Jr., who had personal knowledge of the subject, reported:

> Dr. Haushofer and his men dominate Hitler's thinking. That domination began 17 years ago when the World War general flattered the ex-corporal by paying him visits in prison. Haushofer saw possibilities in the hysterical agitator who had launched an unsuccessful beer-hall revolution. The prison visits became frequent; the distinguished soldier-scientist fascinated Hitler, then finally made him a disciple. The ascendancy has grown as Dr. Haushofer again and again has proved the accuracy of his knowledge and the wisdom of his advice. . . .
>
> It was Haushofer who taught the hysterical, planless agitator in a Munich jail to think in terms of continents and empires. Haushofer virtually dictated the famous Chapter XVI of *Mein Kampf* which outlined the foreign policy Hitler has since followed to the letter.

Haushofer's *Lebensraum* ("living space") theory sought to justify Germany's world conquest by claiming that it was necessary to insure the German people room to preserve and expand their racial community. He developed an intelligence-gathering organization which became the envy and model for all others. He was called everything from "Hitler's idea man" to "the man who will in the end take the *Führer's* place," yet he seems to have kept a very low profile. But there is apparently much more to Haushofer than the geopolitician.

A love affair with the Orient began in 1908, when, as a field artillery officer in the Bavarian army, he was sent to Tokyo to study the Japanese army and to advise it as an artillery instructor. The assignment changed the course of his life. He traveled extensively in the Far East, and added the Japanese, Chinese, and Korean languages to his repertoire of English, French, and Russian. He could not be accused—as other leading Nazis were—of having a provincial background.

His four-year sojourn in the Far East also changed the course of German history. Haushofer was able to make the acquaintance of influential Japanese and to develop a rapport for the culture which helped account later for the German-Japanese alliance. When he returned to Germany in 1912, he had no reason at all to know that the Chinese proverb of which he was so fond, "He who rides a tiger cannot get off," would one day have particular relevance for him.

Haushofer was introduced to Oriental teachings during his stay in the Far East. He had been a devout student of Schopenhauer, and now he could drink directly from the source. He became sufficiently conversant in Sanskrit to translate several Hindu and Buddhist texts, and according to Ravenscroft, he was "an authority on Oriental mysticism . . . concealing the other side of his nature and activities as a leader of a secret community of Initiates, and an authority on every aspect of the 'Secret Doctrine.' [He was] in the esoteric stream of satanism through which he sought to raise Germany to the pinnacle of world power."

(The king of Satanists in America today is Anton LaVey, a former circus lion-tamer who greatly admires the Nazis. LaVey's book, *The Satanic Bible*, published in 1969, is dedicated to a puzzling mixture of people, with one entry reading: "To Karl Haushofer, a teacher without a classroom.")

A number of unsupported theories about Haushofer's occult connections are all rejected by his son Heinz. Haushofer *is* known to have had a reputation for precognition, and a belief in astrology. Johannes Tautz adds to these the belief that he belonged to George Gurdjieff's esoteric circle, which was as well versed in the difficult exercises of the Order of Bektashi Dervishes as Sebottendorff was, and that he was also a secret member of the Thule Society. List's publishing house made a German translation of

Gurdjieff's biography. Gurdjieff traveled extensively through Asia, and may have met Haushofer there. A former disciple of Gurdjieff, Louis Pauwels, believes that Haushofer was a member of "one of the most important secret Buddhist societies" and was on a mission to restore the Indo-Germanic race, which he believed had originated in Central Asia, to its former greatness. If he failed in the mission, he would commit suicide in the traditional Japanese manner.

George Ivanovitch Gurdjieff was born in 1872 in the Caucasus region of Russia, of Russian, Greek, and Armenian ancestry. Like Madame Blavatsky, he claimed to have met members of a Hidden Brotherhood while traveling in Asia, and they imparted to him the occult tradition. He started a school, first in Moscow and then in France, where disciples could open up higher levels of consciousness.

An enigmatic figure, he may have been sent to Tibet as a Russian secret agent. He is believed by some people to have been known there as Dorjieff, the name of the man who taught the Dalai Lama. I have been told that there is a striking similarity in early photographs of both men. J. H. Brennan, a writer on occultism, believes that it was in Tibet that Haushofer made Gurdjieff's acquaintance. In any case, whether Haushofer knew him or not, it is clear that Gurdjieff was never a Nazi sympathizer. He and a group of disciples were in Berlin during the height of Nazi power and watched a street parade, which he proceeded to satirize. He was about to be hauled off to prison, but was dismissed as a madman.

All the same, Haushofer may very well have been imbued with the spirit of Gurdjieff's teaching, which held that men are asleep and that great effort is needed for some of them to awaken and become, in effect, supermen. Gurdjieff believed in the legend of Masters of Wisdom, superhuman intelligences who keep a careful watch over the destiny of mankind and intervene whenever human affairs get out of hand. Though this legend is common in Central Asia and the Near East, it is likely that Gurdjieff derived it from the Order of Bektashi Dervishes. As we will see, it recurred in Nazi mythology.

Gurdjieff also believed that he himself was a source of higher energy from which his disciples could draw. He hinted that he was in direct communication with a higher source, through which "the work for which he was responsible would be able to spread and gain strength in the world," and that "an organization of a higher order was being established in the world which would be able to accept only those who had reached such a stage of spiritual development that they were able to generate higher energies." He believed that his work was evolutionary, because it was "against the stream of life," that is to say, "against nature and against God."

Gurdjieff was far from being a Satanist or a racist, but neither was he bound by traditional ideas of morality. There was an air of the trickster about him and he could often play the cruel despot, which would appeal to the totalitarian mentality.

Pauwels, Brennan, and Tautz have linked Haushofer's name with another esoteric group, the Vril Society, or Luminous Lodge, a secret community of occultists in pre-Nazi Berlin. "Vril" derives from the novel *The Coming Race*, which has prophetic overtones. It was written by an English occultist who is better known as the author of *The Last Days of Pompeii*: Baron Edward Bulwer-Lytton. Written in the nineteenth century, *The Coming Race* details a superhuman subterranean race of beings living in huge caves in the bowels of the earth, who have developed a kind of psychic energy—vril—with which they are made the equals of the gods. They plan, one day, to take control of the earth and bring about a mutation among the existing human elite, subjugating, of course, the rest of slavish humanity.

Baron Lytton himself presumably believed that he was a storer of vril. He practiced ceremonial magic and was claimed by Madame Blavatsky to be a Theosophist. Although he had examined mesmerism, he denied that vril had anything to do with animal magnetism. It was electricity whose properties were the same as "the one great fluid" with which all of life was pervaded. His "Vril people" accumulated it through mental and physical exercises resembling yoga.

The Vril Society in Berlin apparently sought connection with the supernatural beings in the center of the world, and practiced the techniques which would eventually strengthen their mastery of the divine energy, so that they would have power over others and over events. They believed that this attempt at mastery was the only thing which gave purpose to existence. Any other activity was meaningless. One day, when the world was transformed, the beings in the center of the earth would emerge and form an alliance with those initiates who had succeeded in adequately preparing themselves.

The Berlin Vril Society was in close contact with an English group known as the Golden Dawn Society, which was, for a time, headed by the Satanist Aleister Crowley, and counted among its members such illustrious people as the poet William Butler Yeats.

The Golden Dawn Society created an even more exclusive inner group than its competitors, the Theosophists, with admission by invitation only, rule by secret chiefs who were discarnate spirits existing only in the astral plane, the practice of ritual magic, and the use of meeting rooms unknown to outer-order members. Such elitism made it the prototype of other magical groups throughout the continent.

The swastika was a key symbol to Golden Dawn, as it had been to Madame Blavatsky. She had incorporated it into a mystical brooch which she wore. Aleister Crowley had written about it in a tract published in 1910, and he later claimed that the Nazis had stolen the sacred swastika from him.

Haushofer returned to his native country in 1912, and advanced to the rank of general in World War I. He developed a reputation for clairvoyance, predicting, according to Pauwels, "the hour when the enemy would attack, the places where shells would fall, storms and political changes in countries about which he knew nothing."

Rudolf Hess was made his aide-de-camp. It was to remain a lasting relationship. Hess often referred to his old commander as a Secret Chief.

Haushofer the geopolitician is a much more familiar and comprehensible figure than Haushofer the Secret Chief. With his Roman nose and patrician bearing, he made an imposing professor at war's end. He had already distinguished himself in formulating ideas which were well received by the nationalists and Pan-Germans. At the University of Munich, he taught that "war is the father of all things" and that Japan and Germany had a common destiny: to appropriate more "living space" from other nations. He moved quite easily from military affairs to geopolitical statecraft, making good use of his Far Eastern travels. Munich, the center of revolutionary conspiracies, was the perfect intellectual climate for the father of geopolitics. His disciples and pupils slavishly followed his theories and style, and evolved a strategy of German world conquest which presently had a unique opportunity of fulfillment.

His most famous disciple was Rudolf Hess. He followed Haushofer to the University of Munich and sat at his feet, ardently drinking in the pseudoscientific political theories. He was a frequent visitor to the Haushofer home. Mrs. Haushofer was kind enough to give him English lessons. But the professor described his pupil with merciless accuracy:

He was one student among others, not particularly gifted, of slow intellectual grasp and dull in his work. He was very dependent on emotions and passionately liked to pursue fantastic ideas. He was only influenced by arguments of no importance at the very limits of human knowledge and superstition; he also believed in the influence of the stars on his personal and political life. . . . I was always disconcerted by the expression of his clear eyes, which had something somnambulistic about it. . . .

Presumably, the professor was able to effect a change in his student, because he later claimed that it was only Hess who really understood his theories.

On Haushofer's visits to Landsberg, his geopolitical theories were eagerly discussed by all three men, and incorporated into *Mein Kampf*. Hess always remained loyal to both masters.

As for Hitler, he was released first, and wailed to Hanfstaengl about Hess, "*Ach, mein Rudi, mein Hesserl*, isn't it appalling to think he's still there?"

The common experience at Landsberg may have sealed a mystical brotherhood between the two men. Both Hitler and Hess were practiced in occult exercises. In the relatively isolated conditions of their prison room, they could have surrendered to the Grand Work of calling forth untapped powers in themselves. Hanfstaengl believed that Hitler's mind had become "impregnated with the limited doctrines of the Hess-Haushofer coterie" and that Hess had contributed to his "gradual divorce from reality with the inception of the *Führer* cult." Before the Putsch, *Heil* was just an old Austrian custom which the Nazis had appropriated as a way of saying "Good day." After the Putsch, Party people "Heil Hitlered" as a sort of password.

Hess kept his job as secretary on his return from prison, only now it was secretary of the Nazi party. After 1932, when the Nazis came to power, he was made deputy leader, second in command under Hitler. He controlled the central political organization of the Party, supervised and coordinated policy throughout Germany, and was in charge of at least nineteen departments of the government. He was not popular with the other Party people. Kurt Ludecke refers to him as a "notorious" homosexual, and claims he was known as "Fraulein Anna."

He had married at Hitler's suggestion, and according to Goebbels' wife, for years Frau Hess announced that they were about to have a child, because some prophet had foreseen it. They consulted cartomancers, astrologers, and other magicians, who urged on them combinations of drinks and potions, until in the end a son was born. To commemorate the occasion, all the district leaders were urged to make an offering of a sack of earth from their respective districts. The earth was poured under the baby's cradle, as a symbol of his beginnings on German soil. As district leader of Berlin, Goebbels speculated on whether he ought not to have sent a Berlin paving-stone.

Hess was a man hungry for faith and ready to place it in pseudosciences like astrology, homeopathy, and every manner of divination. His fate was ruled entirely by the stars, by the pronouncements of soothsayers, by animal magnetism, the swings of pendulums, and terrestrial radiations. Demons had a terrible reality for him. Hanfstaengl says that Hess was considered

> highly peculiar and went in for vegetarianism, nature cures and other weird beliefs. It got to the point where he would not go to bed without testing with a divining-rod whether there were any subterranean watercourses which conflicted with the direction of his couch. His wife used to complain: "I have as much experience out of our marriage as a candidate for confirmation."

Himmler's Finnish physiotherapist, Dr. Felix Kersten, recalls finding Hess in bed under a huge magnet swinging over him from the ceiling. There were twelve other magnets under his bed, to draw harmful substances out of his body and restore his strength.

Still, Hess was a valuable man to the Party, probably for the reason stated in a character study published in *Das Reich*: "Hess can be silent and keep secrets."

Meanwhile, Hess's original master, Haushofer the geopolitician, was soon transformed into elder statesman. He was made president of the German Academy and of the People's Organization for Germans Living Abroad, and became an important member of the Academy of German Law, which originated the legislation binding on conquered countries. Most impressive of all was his job as director of the Institut für Geopolitik of the University of Munich. After Hitler came to power, he saw to it that Haushofer received unlimited funds for the expansion of his Institut. His was the head which conceived of the plan by which Germany was to conquer the world.

He had long believed that Germany would give birth to a leader who would rule the earth; and astrological predictions had convinced him that this leader would accomplish his mission in an alliance with Japan. He often had premonitions, upon which he acted. He convinced Hitler that the Institut must find out everything about its enemies: strengths, weaknesses, impending famine, religious sensibilities, the personalities and tastes of officials, the morals and corruptibility of even minor bureaucrats, the views of opinion makers. To collate, sift through, and interpret all this material on every country in the world, Haushofer enlisted a staff of more than a thousand students, historians, economists, statisticians, military strategists, psychologists, meteorologists, physicists, geographers, and other specialists, working in Germany and abroad.

The researches apparently paid off. When, in 1938, the General Staff was worried that France would mobilize if Germany invaded Czechoslovakia, Haushofer assured them that it neither could nor would. He turned out to be right. He argued that Poland could be conquered in eighteen days. The military disagreed. They feared their armored trucks would bog down in the Polish mud. Haushofer said it was not likely to rain. It did not. The General Staff didn't believe Germany should invade Norway. Haushofer prophesied that it would be easy. The military wanted to invade France when war first started. Haushofer urged that they wait until German propaganda had made its full impact on the people. He also dictated when the campaigns in Africa and the Balkans would begin. It was his idea that the Nazis make temporary friends with Russia, despite widespread anxiety about collaborating with the Communists. He wooed Latin America for its usefulness against America.

The Nazis tried to keep foreign investigators from finding out how elaborate their new geopolitical machine was. They deliberately led outsiders to believe that they were not themselves taking it seriously, and the deception worked. Deprecatory remarks were made about Haushofer's use of such phrases as the "demoniac beauty of geopolitics," the "Nordic Japanese," "the almost telepathic sensitivity of oceanic nations to foreign dangers." *Time* called his theory "one of history's greatest hoaxes—a vast nonesuch of propaganda for luring Germans to the idea of world domination. . . . Mysticisms, race theories, phony 'cultural' conceptions. . . ." But some observers believed that Haushofer's thinking dominated Hitler's. Even American thought was influenced. Said Hans W. Weigert in *Foreign Affairs*, July 1942: ". . . the highest eulogy a political writer could earn was to be called 'the American Haushofer' . . . colleges all over the country hurried to organize 'Institutes of Geopolitics.' "

He became the geopolitical adviser to Japan, as well, and his house was the meeting-place for Japanese diplomats to come and talk over their alliance with German diplomats.

His eldest son, Albrecht, was also a geopolitician, and occupied the Chair of Political Geography at the University of Berlin. He worked closely with the Foreign Office, and was made Joachim von Ribbentrop's assistant.

Father and son kept up close contact with British members of the upper class—Golden Dawn people, according to Jean-Michel Angebert, a French writer on occultism. Once war broke out, though, there was no longer any way to communicate. The elder Haushofer used his influence with Hess to try to convince Hitler to make peace with England. The same mystical thinking which advised the German army to enlarge the living space of the Third Reich "by moving out from a powerful territorial hub and by accomplishing this conquest progressively, step by step, following the accelerating movement of a spiraling dextrogyre [clockwise rotation]" urged Hess, in the spring of 1941, to embark on an adventure which was to make him the most ridiculous figure in the Third Reich.

The Haushofers had planned for some time a personal meeting between Hess and the Duke of Hamilton, a good friend of Albrecht's. The duke had the ear of Prime Minister Winston Churchill and King George VI. If he could be instrumental in passing on a German peace proposal, it would be worth risking a secret rendezvous. The elder Haushofer told Hess that he had two dreams on two separate occasions. In one, Hess flew a plane to an important destination. In another, Hess walked along the tartan-tapestried halls of a splendid castle (the Duke of Hamilton happened to be Scottish). Twenty-four years earlier, Haushofer's premonitions had been celebrated for their accuracy. Hess was now ready to fly whenever the stars were propitious.

He took off for Scotland alone on May 10, 1941, in a Messerschmitt that had been especially designed for him, with just a few possessions, including visiting cards from each of the Haushofers, an assortment of homeopathic pills, a small hypodermic syringe, and a letter addressed to the duke. Whether or not Hitler knew his plans, if not the specific date of his departure, is still a matter of hot debate.

Hess landed in Scotland, but that was the only part of the trip which went as he and the Haushofers would have expected. The British government did not leap at his peace offer. The German government had to denounce him as mentally deranged, which caused it quite a bit of embarrassment, since Hess had been in a position of authority, with no one questioning his sanity. Hess remained an uncomfortable subject in both countries. British cabinet ministers sealed their lips so tightly that one Londoner quipped: "Never has so much been kept from so many by so few."

The British would not allow Hess to go home, warning that he would be done in by his compatriots if he did. Hess sent Professor Haushofer a birthday greeting:

> Do not worry over me. You, less than anyone, need do this. That my present situation is not exactly agreeable goes without saying. But, in time of war, we have to put up with many things that are not agreeable.

> Let the waves like thunder break,
> Be your very life at stake;
> May you crash or may you land
> E'er as your own pilot stand!

> That I crashed is not to be denied, and it is equally certain that I was my own pilot! In this matter I have nothing with which to reproach myself. It was I who took the controls. You know as well as I do that the compass which guides our affairs is influenced by forces that are infallible—even when we know them not. May those forces be favorable to you in the years to come!

In the event, the "forces" proved no more favorable to Professor Haushofer than to Hess himself.

Not only were hospitals and streets named "Hess" ostentatiously changed after his unsuccessful attempt to end the war, but there was a wholesale routing of astrologers, seers, mediums, and nature therapists.

Hess, meanwhile, grew increasingly paranoid. He was being hypnotized by the Jews, he complained. Furthermore, so were Churchill, Secretary of State Anthony Eden, and the king of Italy.

Karl and Albrecht Haushofer fell from grace. A letter from Martin Bormann to Alfred Rosenberg dated June 17, 1942, suggests that the *National Socialist Monthly* gave the professor too much publicity, and that this should not happen in the future.

Albrecht Haushofer participated in a coup d'état against Hitler on July 20, 1944. The Führer escaped death. Karl Haushofer was sent to Dachau,

Albrecht to Moabite prison. Before his execution, Albrecht composed eighty sonnets, entitled *Sonnets from Moabite*, some of which have become renowned. The collection was in his hands when he was shot on a street in Prussia. Sonnet 39 is called "Guilt":

I should have seen my duty sooner and should have dared with louder voice to name as evil the thing my judgment knew as evil but held too long unspoken. . . . I deceived my own conscience. I lied to myself and others. I early understood the whole sequence of the misery to come.

Sonnet 38 is called "The Father":

In Father's life, the die is cast.
Once it was in the power of his will
To push the demon back into his cell.
My father held the seal and broke it.
He did not sense the breath of evil
And out into the world he let the devil.

After the war, an American was sent to interrogate Karl Haushofer for the Nuremberg War Crimes Trials, and he confessed that Hess had been his favorite pupil. But Karl Haushofer never testified, for he committed suicide in the traditional Japanese manner.

Hess did testify at Nuremberg. The other leading Nazis believed his presence at the trial was a disgrace. He barely seemed to listen, and often dozed. It was as if he were operating on another level of reality.

From 1947, he has been Prisoner No. 7 at Spandau in Berlin. He practices yoga regularly, and though he writes to his wife and son, he says he does not want to see them because it would make the rest of his life sentence too unbearable.

His wife keeps a room for him in a mountain chalet which she manages. "My husband's mouth is closed," she says. "He cannot utter the final word about his deed."

Though she has not seen him since the day he left for England, they are never apart. Says Mrs. Hess:

Telepathy, astrology and his letters keep us together. . . . My husband and I are in constant telepathic contact. People frequently turn up here that I have not seen for years, and inevitably in Rudolf's next letter there are questions about these very visitors. My husband and I receive and send to each other in this way.

CHAPTER 8

Atlantis, the Home of the Master Race

Some say the world will end in ice. . . .

—Robert Frost

Science hasn't yet been able to give us a completely satisfactory answer to the question of how the universe came to be. The occultists are much bolder. From time to time, they have advanced different theories—always colorful—about the origin of the world and of human beings. The Nazis favored the occult cosmology of an Austrian named Hans Hoerbiger.

Born in 1860 to a poor family in Carinthia, Hoerbiger became a blacksmith's apprentice as a youth, and when he scraped together enough money, studied mechanics in Vienna. Eventually, he became a mechanical engineer and inventor. As a boy, he was fond of lying out of doors at night and gazing up at the sky, and the intuition came to him that the moon was an ocean of ice. He extended the vision as a young engineer, in the instant when he saw molten steel poured onto snow and the ground explode violently. He took this as a microcosm for the kind of cataclysm that might have given birth to the universe. In the next two decades, he explored the tension between cosmic ice and fire, which culminated in the publication of a 772-page book, *Glazialkosmogonie*, in 1913.

The "world-ice theory" (*Welteislehre*) is that the universe came into existence when a gigantic chunk of cosmic ice collided with the sun, causing an explosion whose continuing aftermath explains the Great Deluge, the Ice Age, and the differentiation of races. This glacial cosmology went so far as to offer an entirely new theory about the origin of the moon—one which bears a striking similarity to Gurdjieff's. The moon, said Hoerbiger, was originally an independent planet, circling the sun in an independent orbit. It eventually trespassed on the earth's orbit, becoming earth's satellite. The present moon, Hoerbiger continued, was not the first to be captured by the earth; primary, secondary, and tertiary moons had already collided with our planet, and the present moon, captured about thirteen thousand years ago, will eventually crash into the earth too, billions of years hence.

Hoerbiger's ideas were happily pounced upon by occultists, with good reason. He believed that on the three previous occasions when the moon had collided with the earth, the catastrophes which resulted were recorded in the legends about the Flood, about the lost continent of Atlantis, and about the Twilight of the Gods.

Atlantis has always been the favorite place of all occultists. According to ancient tradition, it was a large island in the Atlantic Ocean. Plato, in *Timaeus*, described it as larger than Libya and Asia Minor combined. In *Critias*, he spoke of it glowingly as a powerful nation which later was completely engulfed by the sea.

Whether the continent of Atlantis ever really existed or was the product of human imagination, it has provided ample occasion for speculation. To occultists, it became associated with man's search for hidden wisdom. The supposed Atlanteans, like the Vril people, presumably developed supernormal powers. They were the models upon which esoteric groups patterned themselves, usually according to a blueprint envisioned by their masters in a trancelike state. Atlantis provided these groups with many hours of lectures and workshops, and thousands of books have been written about it—amazing, when you consider that the only original references to it occur in the two works of Plato, *Timaeus* and *Critias*. In neither of these works, moreover, does Plato claim to have firsthand information. One of his characters merely quotes the Athenian jurist Solon. We are never sure whether this is an accurate account of Solon's belief or merely a literary convention.

The latest theory, of course—and this, too, has been disputed—holds that Plato's Atlantis may have been confused with the real Aegean island of

Thera, devastated by a tremendous volcanic explosion in about 1500 B.C. Enthusiasts have sought Atlantis in all sorts of unlikely places. The German völkisch occult groups placed it in Thule, the northernmost part of the earth, and made it the original home of the Aryan master race. They were delighted to have Hoerbiger explain why that home had disappeared.

The glaciers caused by the last falling moon, when they melted, engulfed the whole Atlantean civilization in a deluge, memories of which exist in the legends of all people. This was the fall of man; from this period he degenerated. The occult tradition teaches that some wise and powerful members of the highly developed race went underground and saved themselves from the Great Flood.

Disciples of Hoerbiger also were pleased to point out that the age of giants, set forth in myth and legend, was fully explained by his theory. When a satellite approaches nearer to the earth, the gravitational pull of the earth becomes greater, tides become stronger, and, as Peter Kolisimo explains in *Timeless Earth*,

> as a second consequence, human beings and creatures in general will become taller. . . . this is the only possible explanation of the huge species of plants and animals that have existed on earth, and of a race of men sixteen feet tall. The increase of men's stature, and likewise of their intelligence, is also due, according to this theory, to an increase in the intensity of cosmic rays.

Hoerbiger believed that cosmic events recur. The Ice Age, which seemed to him to recur in cycles of six thousand years, was about to come again. Only this time, supermen who had learned to control cosmic fire and ice would have the option to stop the cycle and make their civilization immortal.

But Hoerbiger was not all cosmic ice and fire. Indeed, his metaphysics also took in the view that there was a world apart from this one, where the laws of cosmic ice were not operable.

The Judeo-Christian notion of primitive man slowly inching his way up to civilization did not accord well with the völkisch Hoerbigerians. To them, it was precisely the other way round: Moons ago, Aryan men had created a marvelous civilization which had been destroyed by the Ice Age; we had yet to approach their splendor. Traces of the lost paradise existed, for those who had eyes to see, in ancient giant monuments, statues, and complex mathematical and engineering constructions.

Hoerbiger was one of many in the scientific community who aligned themselves with the Nazis. After World War I, Jewish scientists and scholars were more readily accepted into the universities, since the republic no longer allowed them to be arbitrarily excluded. The increase in Jewish participation in major universities, along with the anti-Semitic propaganda, accounted for the push among German scholars and scientists to "purge" the Jews and thus advance their own careers. Some, of course, were not just opportunistic, but really believed the völkisch arguments.

Hans Hoerbiger was at the height of his fame in 1925 when he issued a declaration to Austrian and German scientists:

You must choose, and right now, whether you want to be with us, or against us. While Hitler cleans up politics, Hans Hoerbiger will take care of the false sciences. The doctrine of the eternal ice will herald the regeneration of the German people. Watch out! Come over to our side before it is too late!

At sixty-five, Hoerbiger had pitted himself against orthodox astronomy. His appeal, obviously, was to emotion rather than reason. With his white flowing beard, very much like that of his fellow Viennese, Guido von List, Hoerbiger, too, played the role of mystical prophet, warning that "objective science is a pernicious invention, a totem of decadence." He sought to replace it with an inspired piercing of the mysteries. Illumination would come intuitively with the development of "higher" consciousness.

In the post-World War I period, Albert Einstein was the most famous scientist in Germany. Hostility toward him increased in direct proportion to his growing fame. German scientists were made acutely aware that he was a Jew, a pacifist, and a radical. His theories posed a threat to some experimental physicists, who saw in them the eventual ascendancy of theoretical physics. His theories were labeled "meaningless" or "unverifiable abstractions," or else he was accused of not being original. Men who championed the National Socialist cause concentrated on him as their chief scapegoat. Hoerbiger was one of these men.

His success as an engineer had set him up well financially, and he started what amounted to a political campaign, trumpeting his visionary theories like a revolutionary agitator. He wanted to wean people away from the "uselessness" of mathematics and to replace it with an enlightened "knowing." His propaganda spread through mass media, tracts, posters, meetings, and lectures. A monthly periodical, *The Key to World Events*, went to German and Austrian Hoerbigerians. His organization published many books, articles, and pamphlets.

Hoerbiger was greatly helped in disseminating his propaganda by Nazi Storm Troopers. Dietrich Eckart introduced Hitler to Hoerbiger's ideas, and it was a meeting of like minds. Both men knew the importance of mythology in the lives of the masses.

The Storm Troopers among Hoerbiger's followers used the same tactics as Hitler in disseminating their fantasies. Other astronomers' meetings were invaded with cries of "Down with the orthodox scientists!" Rivals were proselytized in the streets, handed leaflets which threatened: "When we have won, you and your like will be begging in the gutter." Hoerbiger admonished industrialists: "Either you will learn to believe in me, or you will be treated as an enemy." They were told to have prospective employees sign a statement reading: "I swear that I believe in the theory of eternal ice."

Other scientists, at first, stood their ground and attacked Hoerbiger's theories. Gradually, as Hitler's strongmen helped to swell his pseudoscience into a popular movement, they were silenced. The system meshed well with the temper of the times and was perfectly tailored to Nazi mythology.

Hoerbiger died in 1931, before he could see some of the consequences of his dogma. Hitler Youth were recruited to spread the word. In 1935, Heinrich Himmler, an admirer, established the *Ahnenerbe* ("Ancestral Research") branch of the SS for the purpose of subsidizing researches into occult theories of ancestral origins of Aryanism. He sent the German playwright Edmund Kiss to Abyssinia, to look for supporting evidence for Hoerbiger's theories, and made another Hoerbiger disciple, Dr. Hans Robert Scultetus, head of the Ahnenerbe branch which was to concentrate on weather forecasts resting on the world-ice cosmology. Literature about this cosmology was handed out freely to high-ranking Nazis. A German expedition to Tibet tried to find fossilized remains of giants. Anyone who attacked Hoerbiger was promptly suppressed by the Ahnenerbe.

In 1936, despite rumors that he was a Freemason and a Roman Catholic, Hoerbiger's son, Hans Robert Hoerbiger, was appointed cosmic-ice Führer by Himmler, who insisted that if the theory were shorn of its fantastic elements, which might hurt his flawless reputation, it would be "scientific" enough to constitute a "really Aryan intellectual treasure." A Nazi pamphlet announced that cosmic ice stood in the same relation to Einstein's theory of relativity as the *Edda* did to the Talmud.

No one was in a position to do more for Hoerbiger's cosmology than
Hitler. He promised that when he built his ideal city in Linz, he would
dedicate an observatory to Hoerbiger. After Hitler came to power, a
number of celebrated engineers and scientists succumbed to the cosmic-ice
theory.

One tract drew attention to the natural affinity between the two self-
made Austrians:

> Our Nordic ancestors grew strong amidst the ice and snow, and this is
> why a belief in a world of ice is the natural heritage of Nordic men. It was
> an Austrian, Hitler, who drove out the Jewish politicians, and another
> Austrian, Hoerbiger, will drive out the Jewish scientists. By his own
> example Hitler has shown that an amateur is better than a professional; it
> was left to another amateur to give us a thorough understanding of the
> Universe.

The few times that these two Messianic leaders met, Hoerbiger actually
outtalked Hitler in his harangue against modern science, which not only did
not understand the *why* of anything but had managed to separate man from
the spirit. Jews like Einstein and Freud distinguished themselves in their
fields and at the same time helped to destroy the belief in magic. They were
pacifists in the bargain. Einstein had called World War I "a fateful
misunderstanding . . . an incomprehensible deception," and Freud went
so far as to claim that all war was a mass regression to a primitive state,
writing: "Never has any event been destructive of so much that is valuable
in the commonwealth of humanity, nor so debasing to the highest that we
know."

With Hoerbiger, on the other hand, Hitler was comfortably in the realm
of Wagner and Nietzsche. The magic of myth would be reestablished in
Germany, with its giants and dwarfs, masters and slaves, transgressions,
sacrifices, and punishments.

Hitler took great pride in being the enemy of "Jewish, liberal" science.
He confessed to Rauschning:

> I thank my destiny for saving me from the State-granted privilege of
> acquiring blinkers in the form of a so-called scientific education. I have
> been able to steer clear of many naive assumptions. Now I am reaping
> the benefit. I approach everything with a vast, ice-cold freedom from
> prejudice.

He often expounded on cosmic catastrophe at the dinner table, holding that "we shall never raise the veil between our present world and that which preceded us" unless intuition teaches exact science the path to follow. Hoerbiger, said Hitler, ranked with Ptolemy and Copernicus. His theory that water "is in reality melted ice (instead of ice's being frozen water) . . . amounted to a revolution, and everybody rebelled against" him, proving once again that science grappled "with the spirit of routine."

Hoerbiger was not accepted by the scientific establishment because "the fact is," said Hitler, "men do not *wish* to know."

Hitler based some important decisions on Hoerbigerian premises. For example, cosmic ice experts caused delays, because they were concerned about the delicate balance between fire and ice. They feared a rocket in space might cause a global disaster. (The military head of the first German rocket tests, Walter Dornberger, also relates that the work was delayed for months at a time because Hitler dreamed that no V-2 rocket would reach England. As an occultist, Hitler took his dreams quite literally.)

Hoerbiger's was not the only occult cosmological theory in which the Nazis believed. There was also the theory of the hollow earth, which received support in Germany after World War I. A leading proponent, Karl Neupert, held that the earth was a spherical bubble, with humanity on the inside, not, as commonly supposed, on the outside. In World War II, certain German naval circles tried to apply the hollow-earth theory. According to an article in *Popular Astronomy* in June 1946, entitled "German Astronomy During the War":

They considered it helpful to locate the British fleet, because the curvature of the earth would not obstruct observation. Visual rays were not suitable because of refraction; but infrared rays had less refraction. Accordingly a party of about ten men under the scientific leadership of Dr. Heinz Fischer, an infrared expert, was sent out from Berlin to the isle of Rügen to photograph the British fleet with infrared equipment at an upward angle of some forty-five degrees.

The experiment did not work.

Nor did an earlier one, called the Magdeburg Project, in which an engineer who was connected with the municipal government of that city devised a way of testing the hollow-earth theory by sending up a rocket. As Willy Ley writes in *Rockets, Missiles, and Men in Space*, "it began like a story by Jules Verne. A mentally decrepit 'philosopher' had written a badly printed pamphlet about the true shape of the universe, in which he insisted that the earth *is* the universe, that we live *inside* a hollow globe of the dimensions of the earth, that there is nothing outside that globe, and that the universe of the astronomers is only an optical illusion.'' If the rocket crashed at the opposite end of the earth, that would prove people lived inside a hollow globe. The rocket cost 25,000 marks, and another 15,000 were spent on a city holiday. Several tests ended in disaster. Either the rocket did not get off the ground, or it smashed, or it flew away, never to be seen again.

After the war, Dr. Fischer protested that the Nazis had forced him ''to do crazy things,'' which had taken him away from more fruitful research, such as he was able to engage in later when he helped America to develop the H-bomb.

Teutonic mythology speaks of the end of all things, the twilight of gods and men, when the world will be consumed in flames because the age of evil has come. Winter will follow winter, in a world chained in ice, and then a new age will come, with a regenerating race.

The apocalyptic vision within the occult tradition is similar. The Fall, and the accompanying Flood, are punishments for man's transgressions, and will purge him of sin. After the Deluge, a Second Coming. Hoerbiger and Hitler believed in this mystique. Modern man, in the twentieth century, had a chance to redeem the species. Hoerbiger and Hitler would point the way.

By spring 1944, the Nazis grew desperate. Hitler must have had grave doubts about man's redemption. The turning point had come for them in the Russian campaign of 1941. Advised by Hoerbigerians to expect a mild winter, Hitler did not even provide his troops with adequate warm clothing. The icy winds did not blow away his mystical faith that he could win. The Russian winter was Germany's most serious military crisis, and Hitler would never admit that he had been wrong. The Russian campaign mystified everyone else.

Hitler had promised, in his early days, that Germany would never surrender again. If she could not conquer her enemies, she would drag them down to destruction with her. Once Hitler was convinced that Germany could not be saved, he made good his promise. When the American and Russian troops were outside of Berlin, Hitler ordered all food and clothing stores, all bridges and dams, all military, industrial, transportation, and communication facilities in the whole country destroyed. Any Germans who stood in the way were to be killed.

Albert Speer, nonmystical, one of the few Nazi leaders who could still communicate with Hitler, was horrified at the order. He tried to argue Hitler out of it by appealing to a concern for the future. After all, many of those bridges, highways, and buildings were Speer's own creations, as the chief architect of the Third Reich:

> We must do everything to maintain, even if only in a primitive manner, a basis for the existence of the nation. . . . We have no right to carry out demolitions which might affect the life of the people. . . .

Hitler's response was in keeping with the superman myth:

> If the war is to be lost, the nation also will perish. This fate is inevitable. There is no need to consider the basis of even a most primitive existence any longer. On the contrary, it is better to destroy even that, and to destroy it ourselves. The nation has proved itself weak, and the future belongs solely to the stronger eastern nation. Besides, those who remain after the battle are of little value; for the good have fallen.

The Germans had proved themselves not to be ready yet to become the master race. Hitler's leadership had been wasted on them. They deserved to perish.

Hitler himself committed suicide on April 30, 1945, a deliberately chosen day, according to J. H. Brennan:

> The Dark Initiate had remained true to his black creed to the very last, had arranged his affairs so that even his suicide should be a sacrificial tribute to the Powers of Darkness. April 30 is the ancient Feast of Beltane, the day which blends into Walpurgis Night. It is perhaps the most important date in the whole calendar of Satanism.

CHAPTER 9

The Obedient Man

This combination of ideas offered a solution of sorts to the
difficulty of applying traditional values to existing conditions. . . . he could sustain his belief in the superiority of
the class from which he came simply by equating the values
of his own group with the characteristics of the dominant and
moral man.

—Bradley F. Smith, *Heinrich Himmler: A Nazi in the Making*

A searching study of Heinrich Himmler's early years helps us to understand the kind of mentality which yearned for the return of the Atlantean
age, and which could go on to carry out Lanz von Liebenfels' extermination policies—all the while considering himself a decent human being.

Born on October 7, 1900, the second son of a Bavarian professor who
became tutor to the son of the prince of Wittelsbach, Himmler grew up in
the Catholic faith. At nineteen, he was earnest enough about his religion to
have noted in his diary an internal conflict over a common fraternity
practice: "During the sermon I had to endure an inner struggle more
serious than any before. The dueling business constantly keeps cropping
up. In the evening I prayed. I had, of course, earlier partly overcome it.
God will continue to help me to overcome my doubts."

He must have decided that God was not opposed to dueling, because he
regularly practiced it. Two decades later, as *Reichsführer SS*, he expressed
no such qualms over the Jewish massacre.

His diary entries recorded in meticulous detail the exact times of arrival and departure of buses and people, and the number of swims he took, banal impressions of books he read, pointing to a pedantic, assiduous character, prone to pontificating. He was a collector of stamps and secrets. He took it upon himself to spy on his elder brother's fiancée, going so far as to hire a private detective to gather incriminating evidence of her disloyalty and succeeding in ending the betrothal.

Once he left the safe haven of his snug middle-class family, his rigid character structure could not bend to the raw winds blowing through Germany. Never a careful thinker, he anguished over the impossibility of finding a respectable niche in the conventional society which gave him comfort. He had been an officer candidate during the war, but when it was over, there were rumors about attacks on officers in Bavaria by Communist revolutionaries. Himmler wrote to his parents, urging them to send civilian clothes so that he could travel unmolested. He also begged them: "Buy all of the coal you can and also all the food, even if you have to buy it by the pound. In 14 days there will be no more coal and no more electric light. . . . Father, you must join the *Bayerisch Volkspartei*, it is the only hope." A postscript, only for his father's eyes, cautioned: "Don't let mother go out alone at night. Not without protection. Be careful in your letters. You can't be sure."

In self-defense, Himmler slowly adopted more and more of the ideology of the radical right, to the distress of his moderate family. Sentimental novels extolling the traditional virtues gave way, in his reading, to vitriolic accounts of the origin of World War I. Like Sebottendorff, they blamed Germany's troubles on a Jewish-Freemasonic world conspiracy. The world-conspiracy theoreticians were themselves beginning to assume the proportions of a world conspiracy.

Some Catholics had long supported the view that Freemasons and Jews were liberal and potentially dangerous to the old order, but Himmler more and more withdrew from identification with the church which, though conservative, was not fanatical enough. He read the "hate" literature with delight, making terse comments in his diary:

A book that explains everything and tells us whom we must fight against next time. It is true and one has the impression that it is objective, not just hate-filled anti-Semitism. Because of this it has more effect. These terrible Jews. Even an initiate is shaken when he reads all this with

understanding. If only some of the eternally blind could have it put
before their eyes.

Writers like Fritsch, Chamberlain, and Gobineau helped him to justify
his own frustrations, while the whole culture's increasing infatuation with
spiritualism made it possible for him to bridge the gap between the death of
the old religious faith and his personal longing for evidence of the existence
of the supernatural.

The books he read signified a deep involvement with and leanings
toward spiritualism and the occult. He labeled occult theories "unbeliev-
ably deep and significant" and particularly enjoyed Karl du Prel's *Der
Spiritismus* ("Spiritualism") because it "really lets me believe in
spiritualism and introduced me to it correctly for the first time."

He was impressed by the arguments for transmigration of souls in a book
on life after death, and noted that it gave him "meaningful new grounds"
for believing in it. This interest in and sympathy with the occult endured
throughout his life. Without it, his role as Reichsführer SS would have
been played out quite differently.

As in the case of Lanz and Hitler, his occultism was bound up with
eroticism. To all three, sexuality was decadent, and the loose morality of
Western Europe after the war seemed to them to travel like a plague, spread
by the "decadent" people, namely, the Jews. They believed Jews were
bestial in their passions, corrupting pure German womanhood and making
all women join the radical cause of feminism. They also saw the Jews as
cunning, practical pimps and pornographers, able to profit materially from
prostitution and from the growing interest in "filth." These were popular
völkisch themes, and Himmler accepted them.

Right after World War I, Himmler was in contact with a number of
Bavarian völkisch groups which were working to get rid of the republican
government. In 1923 he joined the Free Corps, and he must have enjoyed
the sense of participating in a grand design which was to lead Germany
back to greatness. He was welcomed into the Nazi party because, as his
superior, Gregor Strasser, put it, "the fellow's doubly useful—he's got a
motor-bike and he's full of frustrated ambition to be a soldier." Himmler
soon realized that he had a penchant for secret service.

When, in 1925, the SS (*Schutzstaffel*) was formed as a special
bodyguard for Hitler in each district, Himmler was put in charge of his
local unit. It brought him little glory at first. Its petty duties included
soliciting for Party newspaper subscriptions. But in 1927, when the SS

Order was nationalized, Himmler, because of his demonstrated adminis-
trative abilities, was made deputy leader, and in 1929, Reichsführer SS.
The nature of the organization changed. It became a central bureaucracy
for dispensing terrorism, an elitist political police, giving Himmler powers
second only to Hitler. What fitted Himmler for the job were his skill at
pigeonholing people and assigning categories to them, and especially, the
rigid personality defenses he had developed as a student. As Bradley Smith
has pointed out in his biography, "the pose of omniscient hardness" which
he developed early made it possible for him to overcome his awkwardness
in social encounters and to impose himself on others, despite his lack of
charisma. His "social mask" became a weapon habitually used to make
others subordinate to his wishes. Thus, despite his colorlessness, he was
able to compel his Black Guards to go against their own standards of
morality and justify horrifying murder tactics as utopian idealism. He said
proudly of his black-uniformed SS: "I know that there are many people in
Germany who feel sick when they see this black tunic; we can understand
that and do not expect to be beloved by overmany people."

Sometimes he saw his Black Guards as an elite cadre of Teutonic
warriors, and sometimes as medieval knights protecting their lord, Adolf
Hitler. Himmler's interest in the Germanic past and in the Middle Ages
went back to his youth, when he used to spend summer vacations looking
for ancient stones and artifacts, a hobby he learned from his father.

His belief in the transmigration of souls led him to think he was the
reincarnation of the tenth-century German king Heinrich I the Fowler, with
whom he communicated in his sleep. In 1937, he had the monarch's bones
dug up and placed in the crypt of Quedlinburg Cathedral, after a holy
procession. He chose the town of Quedlinburg, in the Harz Mountains,
because it had been founded by the king. Himmler invited Germans to
make a pilgrimage to the tomb to honor Heinrich the Fowler. Yearly, on
July 2, the date of the king's death, Himmler held a midnight ritual in the
clammy crypt. One of the great charms which the medieval monarch had
for Himmler was his anti-Slav crusade. On the thousandth anniversary of
Heinrich's death, Himmler stood before *Wehrmacht* officers and braided
and medaled SS dignitaries and pledged to continue the crusade for German expansion in the east. It was not clear whether he was really talking
about himself or about his namesake when he praised him.

Like List and Lanz, Himmler was obsessed with the secret medieval
society called the Order of the Teutonic Knights. There, a candidate had to
prove pure noble German ancestry for eight generations on both sides of the

family tree. Himmler, in creating a secret order suitable for a mass society, naturally dispensed with the idea of social or economic aristocracy and made the whole Aryan race aristocratic, an idea which List and Lanz had popularized before him. He admired the rigid organization of the Teutonic Knights, and the strictness of their rules. But he must have admired their secrecy above everything else, given his personal propensity for secrets. Even in his brief stint as orderly-room clerk in the army's officer candidates' school, he had collected odd bits of personal information about his fellow cadets, as if in apprenticeship for the job of secret police chief which lay in his future. A few years later, Gregor Strasser laughed him to scorn when he heard about this, asking: "Whatever use do you suppose will derive from knowing who did fatigue duties for insubordination in the 119th Bavarian Infantry Regiment in 1919?" To which Himmler replied: "One never knows."

Himmler was so fanatical a spy that he noted about Party members: "Schwarz was playing *Mendelssohn* on his gramophone when I arrived. It is as well to know of Semitic sympathies." And: "I noticed in [Mucke's] bookcase a copy of Chamberlain's *Foundations of the 19th Century*. He is well chosen for the Führer's personal troop." And about citizens in general: "In the fishmonger's there was a man who mentioned in a low voice to his wife that he suspected treachery in the ranks of the Party. I made it my business to find out his name from the shopkeeper. Such information might be useful in the future."

Himmler knew what a powerful motivation a secret order, with difficult rules and a hierarchical structure, could be; its mere existence held members together in a common bond, subject to the same vows of silence on certain questions.

In trying to create a new Order of Teutonic Knights out of his SS, Himmler was also mindful of the power of the Jesuits. According to his assistant, Walter Schellenberg, he deliberately built the SS organization on the principles of the Society of Jesus, using their statutes and spiritual exercises. In fact, Himmler was called "the Black Jesuit" by his enemies and compared with the order's founder, Ignatius Loyola, by Hitler, who was pleased to have his fanatical devotion.

Schellenberg testified at the Nuremberg Trials that Himmler had

the best and richest library on the Jesuit Order, whose literature he perused at night for years. Thus he built up his SS organization according to Jesuit principles. Its basis was the constitution and the exercises of Ignatius de Loyola: Its supreme law was absolute, blind obedience. . . . Himmler himself, as SS General, was the Order's General Commander. In Westphalia, near Paderborn, he kept a medieval castle, the Wevelsburg, which served, so to say, as the SS monastery. . . . The roots of this attitude . . . go back to his father's education and his severe Catholic conduct of life.

The essential principle which Himmler borrowed from the Jesuits was the oath of absolute blind obedience. In this, he outdid the Jesuits. Though he sought to eliminate all competition to his own esoteric order and officially abominated the Jesuits, they and the SS had a common enemy.

This enemy was the Freemason, who, in his resistance to the dogmas of Original Sin and Grace, in his tolerance and humanism, became the symbol of the Enlightenment, with its belief in the possibility of human perfectibility on earth. His was a rival universal superstate which threatened to replace the less flexible Catholic Church. It was rumored that the Jesuits had destroyed the eighteenth-century Order of the Illuminati by infiltrating the group, a mystical association started by Adam Weishaupt, a former Jesuit student, and diverting it from its original aims. The same suspicions were circulated about Jesuit intrigue in Masonic lodges. The introduction of hierarchical "higher degrees" into Freemasonry was scorned by some Masons as evidence of a Catholic spirit. There were papal bulls of condemnation against the Freemasons, but their power and political influence continued to increase throughout the Enlightenment. The new spirit, which was actually one of reason and an interest in material well-being, was viewed by the Church as a threat to the Faith.

The Jesuits used science in the service of faith, for their aim was never the dispassionate study of astronomy or biology, but the combating of "Satan," from the nineteenth century on, in the guise of materialism.

Germany was the home of the first Jesuit settlement. In Bavaria, particularly, the order stood firm against Lutheranism and held that section of the country, so much so that Munich was called "a German Rome."

The Counter Reformation in Germany was greatly helped by the erection of numerous schools. The zeal of the Jesuits filled the Lutherans with fear and trembling, and a vicious battle ensued; as René Fülöp-Miller points out in *The Power and Secret of the Jesuits*, "it became more and more customary in Germany for men to express the strength of their religious convictions by filthy insults directed against their opponents."

It was in Bavaria, too, that the Jesuits introduced their unique system of "spiritual exercises," reporting to the Pope: "No small benefit has accrued from the Exercises. Some who were falling away are now strengthened, and some who had fallen away are now restored." The exercises spread widely among the Bavarians, adapted to the working classes, under the directive never to "lay too heavy a burden on a too little enlightened spirit or a too weak heart." An "exercise house" was created in Munich, where an efficient lay apostolate was produced.

The spiritual exercises of the Jesuits are designed to awaken the natural powers of the will and connect them with the divine will; the penitent is enjoined to undergo a rigorous series of pictorial imaginings lasting four weeks, during which time he comes to see, hear, smell, and feel scenes of Heaven and Hell. He strives to converse with Jesus and pictures the Incarnation. In an exercise called "composition: seeing the place," the imagination is used to clothe ideas with a visible form. There are prayers for a definite desire and an exercise called "fixing of the objects," and in the end, the penitent's life is changed. These exercises are considered the foundation of the order.

That Himmler practiced visualization is clear from Walter Schellenberg's account in his memoirs. When General Werner von Fritsch was brought to trial on the false accusation of homosexuality, Schellenberg reports:

> I witnessed for the first time some of the rather strange practices resorted to by Himmler through his inclination toward mysticism. He assembled twelve of the most trusted SS leaders in a room next to the one in which von Fritsch was being questioned and ordered them all to concentrate their minds on exerting a suggestive influence over the General that would induce him to tell the truth. I happened to come into the room by accident, and to see these twelve SS leaders sitting in a circle, all sunk in deep and silent contemplation, was indeed a remarkable sight.

Himmler had derived his Round Table idea from the court of the twelfth-century Holy Roman emperor Frederick Barbarossa. Under the influence of knightly thought compulsion, the object of the Round Table's concentration had to submit his will to theirs.

The student of occultism will recognize in the projection of Himmler's picture the magical view that, through visualization, we can change reality. It is an important trick of the trade. This is how the occultist believes he exercises his power, by holding in his mind a mental picture of what he wishes to achieve.

Despite the fact that Himmler's odd ideas made him a ridiculous figure to his underlings, he ruled over them with an iron hand. In a quieter time, he would have been a harmless crank, cultivating his herb garden, studying astrology, graphology, antiquity, mesmerism. His pursuit of these interests in the midst of and even in the service of the most awful atrocities in history has made some historians suspect that he was mad. He had herb gardens planted right in the concentration camps. His order that prisoners be frozen and then, when near death, placed in bed with prostitutes (non-Aryan) to see if body heat and sexual passion could restore them to warmth was inspired by his belief in animal magnetism, the reciprocal action between all living bodies. Through his decrees to SS men on marriage and procreation, he hoped to create a mutant race of supermen. Under his direction, Jewish and Russian heads were severed and sent, in hermetically sealed containers, to a research center to be analyzed for subhuman traits. Just before the end of the war, with the Reich crumbling, Schellenberg arranged a meeting between Himmler and the Swedish Count Folke Bernadotte, to negotiate a surrender. Schellenberg urged his superior not "to expound his astrological and philosophical theories," but even at that tense moment Himmler could not resist putting aside the urgent talk of peace to lecture for an hour on runes. To the discerning eye, he insisted, the uninterrupted script of the Northmen of the Dark Ages resembled Japanese ideograms. This was evidence that the Japanese, too, were Aryans.

The image that Himmler apparently had of himself was that of an idealistic man of science. Yet it was a piece of role-playing, and one is never sure whether he really deceived himself as well as others with it. As fanatical and earnest as he was in the pursuit of his crazy researches, they were convenient rationales for his ideology, as they were for Hitler. The image of the dispassionate scientific researcher was often distorted. So, for instance, Hermann Rauschning reports a conversation with Himmler, incensed at the audacity of a professor who dared to criticize the Nazi dogma about the origins of the Teutons:

What ideas, he said, these gentlemen got into their heads! . . . if the State or the party had declared that a certain view was regarded as the desired starting-point for scientific research, that view must be accepted simply as a scientific axiom. . . .

"We don't care a hoot whether this or something else was the real truth about the prehistory of the German tribes [said Himmler]. Science proceeds from hypotheses that change every year or two. So there's no earthly reason why the party should not lay down a particular hypothesis as the starting-point, even if it runs counter to current scientific opinion. The one and only thing that matters to us, and the thing these people are paid for by the State, is to have ideas of history that strengthen our people in their necessary national pride.

"In all this troublesome business we are only interested in one thing—to project into the dim and distant past the picture of our nation as we envisage it for the future. Every bit of Tacitus, in his *Germania*, is tendentious stuff. Our teaching of German origins has depended for centuries on falsification. We are entitled to impose one of our own. . . . Prehistory is the doctrine of the eminence of the Germans at the dawn of civilization."

Himmler's views and deeds were not the excesses of madness, though they were not always rational. They owe more to the dissociations of the fanatical occultist than they do to the divided personality. If he spent much of his own time and that of his men in investigating crankish researches, this did not diminish his talents for efficient organization.

If his reality was non-ordinary, it was not because he was crazy, but rather, as his masseur, Dr. Felix Kersten, tells us, because he was "extremely superstitious." He believed in "good and evil spirits" and was "always afraid of an invisible power" to which he would "one day have to give an account of himself." When Dr. Kersten asked him how, with this view, he could do the things he had to do, believing as he did that according to the doctrine of karma his deeds would determine his destiny in his next incarnation, Himmler answered:

You oughtn't to look at things from such a limited and egotistical point of view; you have to consider the Germanic world as a whole—which also has its Karma. A man has to sacrifice himself, even though it is often very hard for him; he oughtn't to think of himself. Of course it's pleasanter to concern yourself with flower-beds rather than political dust-heaps and refuse-dumps, but flowers themselves won't thrive unless these things are seen to. I try to reach a compromise in my own life; I try to help people and do good, relieve the oppressed and remove injustices wherever I can. Do you think my heart's in all the things which have to be done simply from reasons of state? What wouldn't I give to be Minister for Religious Matters like [Bernhard] Rust and be able to dedicate myself to positive achievements only! . . .

Over and over again, Himmler referred to the work of the SS men in concentration camps as sacrifice. It was as though they had to suffer a greater ordeal than their victims. One of his most interesting speeches to his officers sympathizes with this ordeal: "To have stuck it out, and at the same time . . . to have remained decent fellows, that is what has made us hard. This is a page of glory in our history which has never been written and is never to be written. . . ."

Every cause has its idea of sacrifice, calling on the individual to give up his well-being for the sake of something greater. Himmler's idea of sacrifice was influenced by Eastern philosophy. He had read the Bhagavad-Gita, the Vedas, the Rig-Vedas, the sayings of Buddha, the Visudi-Magga, and the Book of Purity, and had learned to practice that detachment from his acts which, while it might seem silly or monstrous to the foolish, was purifying to the wise.

Karma required only that the individual carry on his unavoidable duties, disregarding the consequences. As it is written in the Bhagavad-Gita: "One should not give up the activity to which one is born (*sahajam karma*: the duty incumbent on one through birth, caste, profession), even though this should be attended by evil; for all undertakings are enveloped by evil, as fire by smoke."

The disengagement from the effects of fulfilling one's duties was self-sacrifice.

Himmler was particularly fond of the Bhagavad-Gita, and told Dr. Kersten that he "never moved without it." He prized it for its "great Aryan qualities." He was also an avid student of the *Arthasastra*), Hinduism's anticipation of Machiavelli. This handbook of statecraft reached the West shortly before World War I. It seemed to Christian scholars to embody pagan wickedness, and though it was no more cynical than Machiavelli, it was not redeemed by his Western spirit. The *Kautilya Arthasastra* was especially cherished by Himmler. Here was laid out a crafty system for international espionage in the service of the tyrant state, from which a fanatical Nazi flunky could learn a good deal. Its Oriental despots and warriors were Himmler's people—Aryans. Their amorality accorded well with his own, and could even be linked to the divine essence. The artifices and cunning advocated by the *Kautilya* were nowhere practiced more heartily than in the Third Reich, where hypocrisy and deception were raised to a fine art.

Himmler began more and more to propagate occult ideas among the SS.

When several astronomers were courageous enough to call Hoerbiger's theory an outmoded concept, Himmler answered:

> I advocate unrestricted research of whatever kind and that includes unrestricted research into glacial cosmogony. I intend to encourage that research and in so doing I find myself in the best of company . . . as the Führer, too, is a convinced supporter of this theory so much abominated by scientific hacks. . . . the Ministry . . . must put these opinionated schoolmasters in their place. There are a great many things we should like to see researched, even by non-scientists.

Under his supervision in the SS, a great many things *were* researched. The crank succeeded eventually in having millions of men explore his fanatical notions, sending to their ruin millions more.

CHAPTER 10

The Black Knights

The selection of the new Führer class is what my struggle for power means. Whoever proclaims his allegiance to me is, by this very proclamation and by the manner in which it is made, one of the chosen. This is the great significance of our long, dogged struggle for power, that in it will be born a new master class, chosen to guide the fortunes not only of the German people but of the world.

—Hitler

Though we have not yet learned all of the secrets of the SS and may never learn them, we do know some of them. We know that it was an occult society. This may enlighten us as to how more than a million SS men could change, in the space of a few years, from ordinary citizens to mass murderers. Some of them must have participated in the Final Solution just to get on, in a period when it was surely not easy just to get on. But we cannot fail to comment on the zealousness—the overzealousness—with which most men approached their tasks. Fear of punishment does not quite account for it. There were many options, not picked up, to quietly sabotage the SS machine without detection. One could seem perfectly willing to perform an unpleasant task and yet raise questions as to its efficacy. So, for example, the deputy head of the Nazi Health Bureau, Dr. Kurt Blome, wrote to his superior, Arthur Greiser, on November 18, 1942, about the order to exterminate all the Polish population who were tubercular:

There is no doubt that the method proposed is the simplest and most radical. If there could be an absolute guarantee that the matter would be kept secret, one could stifle any scruples one might have. But I believe complete secrecy to be simply impossible and experience shows that we must work on that assumption. Suppose that according to plan these sick persons are despatched to Germany ostensibly for treatment or cure but in practice do not return; however strict the secrecy, their relatives will one day realize that there is "something not quite in order" here. It must also be remembered that there are large numbers of Polish workers in Germany who will be questioned about the whereabouts of their fellow countrymen; in addition, a number of Germans are related to Poles, either directly or by marriage, and they will get to know of the deportation of these people. Definite information regarding this action will soon filter through and will be seized upon by enemy propaganda. The euthanasia affair showed us the form which this propaganda will take and the methods it will use. Political repercussions may be all the greater in that we are dealing with members of a defeated nation. . . .

I therefore believe that before action begins, these points should be put to the Führer, since in my view he alone is capable of considering all the implications and making the decision. . . .

By this means, Blome caused Himmler to reconsider, and the lives of thousands of Poles were saved.

In order to make sense of the brutal activities of the SS, it must be seen that its members were motivated, for the most part, not by sadism, but by sacrifice in a fanatical utopian cause which suspended normal judgment. Present-day occult groups have improved our understanding of the human capacity for personality change and for expanding the boundaries of endurance. They show us how malleable people are. They give us new insights into how an appeal to idealism and a training for self-sacrifice can prepare people for deeds which transcend individual conscience.

Membership in the SS seemed to present an opportunity to become part of a utopian society—its most vital part. The Nazi revolution, like the Communist revolution, aimed to turn things around, but instead of a class struggle, it was concerned with a racial struggle. A new class would be brought to power, not the old aristocracy, but a new aristocracy, based on the inherent nobility of the Aryan blood. The master race was to be the culmination of a biological evolution. If "inferior" races prevented these goals, the master race would be justified, by the "natural law" of Darwinism, in doing whatever it needed to survive the harsh struggle for existence. This had an immediate appeal to the masses. Sons of middle-class men, like Himmler, who could not even hope, in that gray time of the twenties and thirties, to approach the comfortable standard of living of their fathers, now saw an escape route.

It was not necessarily outcasts or scoundrels who joined the SS, but ordinary people, members of the lower and middle classes, who saw in it a chance to participate in a movement with which they could identify. They were to be the warriors against the enemy. They recognized the enemy. Many of these men had fathers who had read the books of List, Lanz, Fritsch, and Chamberlain and believed in the mystical racist package. The churches, too, had shown sympathy with the völkisch ideas. In school, the future Nazis had been taught by people who had been conditioned by the same *Zeitgeist*. On joining the SS, then, a man had little to unlearn.

As a bulwark against the horror of the future, in which all the avenues of growth seemed to be closed, the organization promised new options. The renunciation of personality which it required of the individual he gladly assented to. For the sake of being part of a utopian society which would usher in a golden age, he was willing to give up personal liberty. He had been told for some time, anyway, that individual liberty was a fiction. Often, it was only the liberty to go down the drain. If, in the process of the SS training, an individual was transformed into a machine, he could justify it with the propaganda that he was on the way to becoming "the new man." As Rudolf Hoess, commandant of Auschwitz, put it: "We were told all the time we were the elect, we were to be the Führer's and Himmler's special instrument for creating a new Reich. They became our conscience, we lost our personal moral self-determination."

There was a feeling that "the Last Days were at hand," that the "subhuman" Jew, Satan in disguise, had to be prevented, by any means, from taking over the world. A crusade of the elect, in absolute obedience to the will of the charismatic Führer, was a "divine mission." As Himmler told the SS:

We shall unremittingly fulfill our task. . . . We shall take care that never more in Germany, the heart of Europe, can the Jewish-Bolshevik revolution of subhumans be kindled internally or by emissaries from abroad. Pitilessly we shall be a merciless executioner's sword for all these forces whose existence and doings we know . . . whether it be today, or in decades, or in centuries.

If Germany after World War I was a man-made jungle, the new man was the natural man, very much at home in the economic and psychic swamp. Encouraged to "think with his blood" and to renounce the bourgeois shackles of humanism, he turned, as Himmler had, from the tender romanticism of knightly deeds and pure fellow-feeling to the savage romanticism of barbaric slaughter. In this, he was the archetypal twentieth-century man, daring to destroy the old forms so that the new could be born. He was a modern warrior, accomplished in technology, who reverted to savagery, so that, in a curious way, he came to embody both rationalism and irrationalism.

These were not the only ambiguities. Though SS men were trained to be the first stage in a superhuman mutation, and already behaved as if they were supermen, they also exhibited a robotlike quality. Fearless and cruel, they were also capable of a cringing subservience to superiors. What was the nature of the order which could contain such paradoxes?

It was an elite society, with strict conditions for acceptance. Himmler himself scrutinized applicants' photographs for an intuition into their breeding. They had to prove that only pure Aryan blood had flowed into their veins for three generations. They had to meet certain requirements of racial appearance, physical condition, and general bearing. Intellectual attainments were not considered. They had to go through innumerable political and physical tests, demonstrate that there were no hereditary imperfections in their families, and be examined for racial purity by a board of doctors, racial specialists, and SS officers. The ratio of height to physique was important:

No one could be under 1.70 meters [5' 7''], and if he were over 1.80 [5' 11''] or 1.85 [6' 1''], although this was in itself gratifying, the height must be balanced by the harmony of the rest of the body—the lower thigh, for example, must be in proportion to the upper. The hands, the gait, the bearing must be those of the desirable SS man, an ideal physical and psychological type on whose specifications they had been working since 1931, said Himmler.

Even underarm perspiration was made a distinguishing characteristic.

If the applicant met the specifications, he was then made a candidate. He had to swear an oath of loyalty, bravery, and obedience unto death to his superiors and to Hitler. An SS lieutenant general had to swear further that he would not favor his own offspring or those of other SS men.

In the prolongation of examination and testing, Himmler copied the Jesuits, with their two-year-long period of rigorous tests and exercises for novices before they allowed them to take the vows of poverty, chastity, and obedience. Before a candidate was allowed to consider himself an SS man, he had to pass through a year-long course to win his sports badge, a period in the Labor Service, and two years in the army. Then, after an intensive course of indoctrination, he had to wait until the following November 9 to become a full member. At 10:00 P.M. in the Nazi shrine in Munich, the acolyte attended a special mystical ceremony binding him to his Führer, who was present. The scene before the Feldherrnhalle was described thus by a Nazi, Emil Helfferich: "Tears came to my eyes when, by the light of the torches, thousands of voices repeated the oath in chorus. It was like a prayer."

Himmler had replaced the Catholic catechism with his own series of questions and answers, which he dinned into each SS man's head, as for example:

QUESTION: Why do you obey?
ANSWER: From inner conviction, from belief in Germany, in the Führer, in the Movement and in the SS, and from loyalty.

Himmler was known as "the Black Jesuit," and created a hierarchical structure with a graded series of privileges, separating the higher orders from the lower orders, with himself as "General of the Order." He understood well the elitist leanings of his men, and their fear of losing their status. Everyone was constantly spying on everyone else, and even the top officers were not exempt from being visited by emissaries who arrived unannounced to see whether things were being done according to regulations. Naturally, then, despite the conditioning these men were daily receiving that they were the hope of civilization, they lived in constant dread of being discovered to be in some way unworthy of such a high calling. As Robert Ley pointed out:

He who fails or actually betrays the party and its Führer . . . will not thereby merely be deprived of an office, but he personally, together with his family, his wife, and his children, will be destroyed. These are the harsh and implacable laws of an Order. On the one hand men may reach to the skies and grasp whatever a man can desire. On the other hand lies the deep abyss of annihilation.

Yet there was a fierce pride in having been chosen for a superhuman task, and the romanticism persisted:

And how they drilled us till we howled with rage—over obstacle courses, crawling through pipes; pack drills and long route marches in the heat, with the taps all turned off so that we could not drink. Yet no one would dream of asking for a transfer, such was the comradeship. One got so that one lost all criticism; one just lived in this life; one was simply an SS man. One lost the thin thread to the parents. There was no other thought than *Kadavergehorsam.*

Kadavergehorsam—cadaver obedience—was achieved not just through fear but through the creation of a religious fanaticism which separated SS members from everyone else. The SS order was a state within a state, not subject to national law, with its own laws, courts, and judges. A curtain separated Himmler's empire from the outside world; other Germans, no matter how lofty their position, could not penetrate it. SS men were discouraged from contact with others. Concentration-camp guards could not be stationed near home, were shifted to new locations every three months, and could never be transferred to street duty.

The SS was a secret society, as the journalist Heinz Höhne observed:

. . . intended to be mysterious, sinister and incomprehensible to the ordinary citizen, like the Order of Jesuits which the SS officially abominated but actually imitated down to the smallest detail. The Lords of this black-uniformed secret Order deliberately cultivated the fear evoked by their mere existence. . . . [Reinhard] Heydrich [deputy chief of the Gestapo] . . . boasted: "The Gestapo, the *Kriminalpolizei* (Criminal Police) and the security services are enveloped in the mysterious aura of the political detective story."

Even as early as 1927, the SS's slogan was: "The aristocracy keeps its mouth shut." Members were not allowed to take part in discussions at Party meetings. They were to remain silent, and refrain from smoking or leaving the room. One of the early orders was:

Even in the face of unjustified criticism, SS men and SS commanders are strictly forbidden to converse with SA [Sturm Abteilung [Storm Troopers] men and commanders or with civilian members of the Party other than as necessary for the performance of duty. Should criticism be voiced in a small gathering, members of the SS will immediately and silently leave the room with a curt comment that the SS carries out Adolf Hitler's orders.

As an early memorandum suggested, the SS was organized to be "a secret Order within the Party to hold the movement together in an iron grip." An inner circle of twelve SS officers of top rank met in secret for conference and meditation in a monastery in Wevelsburg, Westphalia, which Himmler had turned into a castle, refurbishing it at tremendous expense. The town was built on the foundations of a burgh that went back to Charlemagne, and Himmler supposedly searched the province for this castle because he had heard that in the next confrontation with the East, a Westphalian castle would be the only stronghold to survive.

In the 100-by-145-foot dining room, circling a round oak table, each officer-knight sat on a high-backed pigskin chair, a silver plate engraved with his name hanging from the back. Each wore his own coat-of-arms and slept in a room done in period style suitable to a particular German hero—Himmler, of course, choosing King Heinrich I, whose spirit apparently gave him invaluable counsel. Himmler would say, on occasion: "In this case King Heinrich would have acted as follows." Heinrich I was not the only great spirit of the past with whom Himmler was able to communicate. He believed he had the power to call up others and hold conferences with them, but only if they had been dead for hundreds of years.

In the bowels of the castle was a funereal room containing a sunken well and a hollowed-out stone pillar. When one of the twelve top-ranking officers died, his ashes were placed in a cremation urn by the well. His escutcheon was burned on top of the pillar and the smoke would rise above the well, because of a cleverly arranged ventilating scheme.

For a week once a year, Himmler and his twelve Knights of the Round Table, in an atmosphere of secret confinement, gave themselves over completely to mental and spiritual exercises of visualization.

A professor of anthropology at Occidental College in California, C. Scott Littleton, provided me with astonishing details of another SS ceremony which has not been corroborated by anyone else, but which may well be true. A professor friend of his, he claims, saw original Nazi depositions taken for the Nuremberg Trials, but never included in the record, which told of a periodic sacrifice wherein a fine Aryan specimen of an SS man was beheaded and the severed head made a vehicle for communion with Secret Masters in the Caucasus. These beings, presumably, were not believed to be earthly, and were looked to for guidance.

Whether this is true or not, we do know that in schools of instruction at Wevelsburg and other, less completed castles at Sonthofen in Bavaria, Vogelsang in Rhenanie, and Krossinsee in Pomerania, candidates were systematically prepared to participate in atrocities. Each school had its dormitories, refectories, chapel room, meditation cloister, and private cemetery. In Wevelsburg, a library of twelve thousand volumes comprising all of the known literature relating to the cult of race was made available.

René Alleau relates that in each of these schools, men, stripped to the waist and without any defensive weapons, were taught to become hard by such ordeals as fighting off for twelve minutes attack dogs that were unleashed and incited to kill. If the candidates took flight, they were shot. Another gruesome preparation for pitilessness, according to Alleau, consisted of tearing out the eyes of three cats with one's bare hands. Throughout these barbarities, one had to show utter indifference to sorrow.

Officer candidates were often told to pull a pin out of a grenade, balance it on their helmets, and stand at attention until it exploded.

Such training gave men the ability to walk unmoved among corpses. And such ferocities were coupled, in the classroom, with racist educational courses designed to separate the SS man further from the outside world, because they were deliberately anti-Christian and quickly created a climate of neo-paganism. Christian names were replaced with Teutonic names. Christmas was brought forward to the winter solstice and celebrated as Yuletide, which, an SS manual assured, was the

greatest festival of our forebears. They advanced towards the Yule-night with firebrands to liberate the sun from bondage of wintry death, and thought of it as a young hero come to rouse and free them from their death-like sleep. . . . On Christmas eve the main ingredients of festive fare must be carp, roast goose and wild boar—drawn respectively from the sphere of water, air and earth. . . . in view of the fact that [this] is the greatest clan festival—it is becoming customary to . . . exchange ideas about the success of the steadily deepening research into family genealogies.

The cult of ancestors, which Himmler fostered to give his men a feeling of being part of a great continuum, also took in the Germanic forebears of the Middle Ages. Like Lanz's New Templars, SS members delved into the occult mysteries of the Grail legends. All their mystical rituals, says Joachim Fest,

not only conferred a special distinction but also placed them under a special obligation. . . . had the additional purpose of overwhelming those present with a melancholic shudder at his [Himmler's] innate demonism. Over and above this, they were intended to inspire those states of rapture which are so easily transformed into brutal and merciless violence. But none of this belies the initiatory character of these solemn hours, which amounted to a repeated act of consecration and total commitment to a community opposed to all traditional ties, one that seriously demanded "unconditional liberation from the old social world of caste, class and family" and "proclaimed its own 'law' as springing unconditionally from the mere fact of belonging to the new community."

Since the members of this new community were heirs to the old German nobility, it mattered with whom they mated and begot children. The future of the German people depended on it. Himmler laid down elaborate rules for marriage. How he must have enjoyed prying into the most intimate details of his men's lives. Future wives had to pass the same rigorous test for Aryanism as SS men. At christenings, as at deaths, the priest was supplanted by the local SS leader. Every fourth child born to an SS man received a present of a candlestick with the inscription "You are only a link in the clan's endless chain." The breeding catalogs of the order's Race and Settlement Bureau read like one of Lanz von Liebenfels' tracts. Men were urged to have children out of wedlock with racially pure women, and there were special facilities set up for these purposes.

At the height of the war, Himmler had so many of his men and so much money involved in esoteric research projects that it began to seem as if he hoped to turn the tide in Germany's favor by fathoming the secrets of Rosicrucianism and Freemasonry, the occult meaning of Gothic spires and the top hats worn by the boys at Eton, and the symbolism involved in the suppression of the Ulster harp. These projects were all undertaken by the Foreign Intelligence Service.

The most ambitious researches were done by the *Ahnenerbe*, which had a group of financiers called the Circle of Friends, led by Wilhelm Keppler, pay enormous sums for a flight to Tibet to look for traces of a pure Germanic race which might have been able to keep intact the ancient Nordic mysteries. The *Ahnenerbe* also had archeologists digging up all of Europe for remains of Germanic culture. More than fifty departments in this branch succeeded in spending over a million marks ($400,000) on such "vital" matters.

But the most incredible research of all was set up in 1939 in Berlin. An astrologer, Wilhelm Wulff, who was made prisoner of the SS and coerced into working for it, described the Berlin Institute's scientific research center as being used "to harness, not only natural, but also supernatural, forces. All intellectual, natural, and supernatural sources of power—from modern technology to medieval black magic, and from the teachings of Pythagoras to the Faustian pentagram incantation—were to be exploited in the interests of final victory."

In March 1942, the astrologer joined this "very strange company, which included spiritualist mediums and sensitives, pendulum practitioners (dowsers who used a pendulum instead of a dowsing rod), students of Tattwa (an Indian pendulum theory), astrologers and astronomers, ballistics experts, and mathematicians."

Under the direction of a navy captain who believed that British Intelligence was able to find the whereabouts of German U-boats simply by sitting in the Admiralty office in London and swinging a pendulum over a map, noticing when the pendulum would begin to rotate, and radioing a message to British destroyers telling them the exact location of the U-boats, Himmler decided to have his people do the same. (Actually, the British had simply succeeded in breaking the secret German code.)

One member of the German team, Ludwig Straniak, a Salzburg writer and architect, claimed that he could hold a pendulum over a picture of a boat and then "search" the map with the same pendulum. The German Admiralty was impressed, and let him swing. He and others sat for hours on end, day after day, arms outstretched over maps, but, says Wilhelm Wulff, who was also adept in occultism, "the results were, of course, pitiful. Whatever one may think about occult phenomena, it was simply ridiculous to expect that an unknown world could be forcibly opened up in this dilettante fashion and exploited for military purposes." When the experimenters "began to suffer from nervous exhaustion," the project was moved out of Berlin and into "quieter and more salubrious surroundings on the island of Sylt, perhaps on the basis that a little ozone would help the 'vibrations.' "

Wulff, as a student of Vedanta and Buddhist yoga, went on to work with German soldiers, instilling in them "the Zen-Buddhist beliefs which inspired the Japanese."

The pendulum swingers surfaced again in 1943, after Mussolini was arrested by the government of Pietro Badoglio. Although Hitler was most anxious to rescue him, German Intelligence could not find out where he was held captive. The same occultists who had been arrested after Hess's flight were now released and taken to a villa in Wannsee, where Himmler ordered them to use pendulums, clairvoyance, astrology, or any other means to locate the missing dictator. As Schellenberg recounts:

> These séances cost a mint of money because what the "scientists" needed in the way of good food, drinks and smokes was enormous. . . . After a while a pendulum *maestro* said . . . island to the west of Naples. In fact the Duce had first been taken to one of the small Ponza islands that he indicated. It must be stated in all justice that the man had no contact with the outside world at the time of the experiment.

Though this experiment is innocuous enough, it is a further demonstration that an occult climate existed in the SS. Its members could not have accepted the crazy ideology which goaded them into ridding the world of supposed evil by wiping out millions of people if they had not first been turned into robots, methodically and successfully, so that one of their leaders, Robert Ley, could announce to them: "When I look at you my men, I know that the principles on which we mustered you are right. Externally you already look alike and in a short time you will be alike inside as well."

We are learning now, from contemporary cults in America, that the process of turning human beings into robots can actually begin quite innocently. Among SS men, it was so effective that even at the end of the war, they were still able to call their unscrupulous acts sacred deeds.

CHAPTER 11

The Children's Crusade

My teaching is hard. Weakness has to be knocked out of them. In my *Ordensburgen* a youth will grow up before which the world will shrink back. A violently active, dominating, intrepid, brutal youth—that is what I am after. Youth must be all those things. It must be indifferent to pain. There must be no weakness or tenderness in it. I want to see once more in its eyes the gleam of pride and independence of the beast of prey. . . . In this way I shall eradicate the thousands of years of human domestication. Then I shall have in front of me the pure and noble natural material. With that I can create the new order.

—Hitler

Nineteenth-century German youth was not yet hard. It was innocent. And it usually belonged to one or another youth group, whether religious, athletic, nature, cultural, or a combination of these. Some of them built medieval castles in the air. They were all an expression of restlessness and bewilderment, and well they might have been, for Germany, especially after World War I, was a place which was losing its hold on sense and purpose. Young people not only felt estranged from the government, but from adults in general. Though the same could be said of youth throughout Europe, particularly in the middle class, the difference in Germany was that it did not, for the most part, attach itself to the liberal cause, the way youth movements elsewhere did.

The Children's Crusade 105

The German youth movement began at the end of the nineteenth century and was not at all political at first. It was a romantic protest against a society in which young people were superfluous. Middle-class youth had been educated and brought up to believe that they could claim their birthright on coming of age. Work and position would be theirs. In adolescence they experienced the culture shock of Kafkaesque alienation. Meaningful work and the status that went with it were claimed by the lucky few. To the rest, young manhood ushered in a period of drift.

The youth groups filled a vacuum. Everyone seemed to recognize that it was the end of an age, and that the futility and smallness which men now felt would not aid them in getting out of the snares of mechanized modern life. The youth groups, whatever their particular character, had certain things in common: They all promised liberation from artificiality, alienation, and sterility, and wholeheartedly opposed the bourgeoisie, which stood for everything that had failed them. They brought back the romanticism of the Middle Ages. Its simple faith, loyalty, and high-minded love contrasted with the impersonality and decadence around them. But it was not to be all feudal music and peasant crafts. The youth movement early on fell under the spell of third-rate philosophers with extremist notions, men like the occultist Theodor Fritsch; the Orientalist Paul de Lagarde; and Julius Langbehn, who believed he had sufficient magical powers to exorcise the demons from Friedrich Nietzsche, then languishing in an asylum.

Racism became violent and brutal and mixed with occultism through the influence of men like Lanz von Liebenfels and List. Lanz's comic-book heroes appealed to the young. They were larger-than-life and boosted the adolescent egos of their German readers, who could identify with their pure-blooded rage against the despoilers of civilization. List's fantasies were equally flattering. His glorification of Germanic history and deification of nature were bathed in the rosy glow of a sun which symbolized hidden psychic powers. As the historian George L. Mosse made clear in *The Culture of Western Europe*: "These men believed that their ideals possessed a tremendous magnetism for the hopeless, rationalistic world of the present. . . . Some took to the spiritualism of Madame Blavatsky or to the fad for Oriental sects which promised nirvana from the present."

The whole of Germany was swept up in this esoteric wave, and youth more than anyone. The peculiarly nineteenth-century phenomenon, spiritualism, and its more "scientific" variation, Theosophy, in Germany were welded together with a mystical concept of the Volk as a people whose collective "soul" was more than the sum of its parts. This Aryan "soul," Germans believed, united the individual German to his geographical place. Every tree and rock of German soil was holy, and spoke to the people, shaping them and causing their creativity. The intuitive wisdom of which the Aryans, rooted in their land, were capable was hidden from the Jews, those eternal wanderers, who had no organic place of their own and, therefore, tried to usurp the fatherland of others. On this account, the Jew was most comfortable in the city, alienated from nature and the Volk. Spiritualism joined itself to the idea of the Volk, in that nature emitted a vital ether, a life force, with which only the Aryan was in touch. He alone could contact an extrasensory world which would yield up its secrets and give him special powers.

The new romanticism was, above all, irrational, and this seemed to guarantee its easy acceptance. It peddled itself as more substantial than the discoveries of science, because science itself did not claim to understand the dark mysteries of the force which drove nature, whereas Madame Blavatsky and others like her did. List, borrowing her Theosophy, also did. Her "ancient wisdom," transposed by him into Germanic wisdom which had been destroyed by Christianity, could be revived through intuition, and would explain the essence of things. German mystics developed an ideology, a hodgepodge of the occult, racism, and romanticism which, while ridiculous, went down surprisingly well with youth hunting for certainties. Many young people, Walter Z. Laqueur points out in *Young Germany*,

joined one of the many new religious and occult sects whose prophets grew like mushrooms in the *völkisch* camp between the First and Second World War. Of such were Mathilde Ludendorff's [the general's wife] *Tannenberg Bund*, Arthur Dinter's group, the Asgard Circle, or Gustav Müller's sect, which believed that the human soul was an amalgamation of three or four animal souls ("according to reliable reports from beyond"), and that the planet Mars was the place where man first appeared.

To children whose fathers had been killed in the war, the leaders of these groups became surrogates. To adolescents disturbed by a fragmented society, they offered solidity. To students who knew that nothing awaited them upon graduation from school, they offered immersion in the group. To alienated youth drifting into dreary, unfriendly cities, they offered companionship. To young people bewildered by the intricacies of sex, they offered the solution of rigorous puritanism. To children who could no longer believe in the God of their fathers, they offered a new, modern God. To those thirsting for absolute meanings, they provided absolute answers. As one participant put it (in E. Y. Hartshorne's *German Youth and the Nazi Dream of Victory*):

> Mysticism and everything mystical had dominion over us. It was in our ranks that the word *Führer* originated, with its meaning of blind *obedience* and devotion. The word *Bund* arose with us, too, with its mysterious undertone of conspiracy. And I shall never forget how in those early days we pronounced the word *Gemeinschaft* ["community"] with a trembling throaty note of excitement, as though it hid a deep secret.

He goes on more objectively:

> The tragedy of the appeal of this mysticism to the youth of the post-war period was that it offered them a dreamy haven of refuge from the pressing problems of the day.
>
> A significant proportion of cultured idealistic youth was thus, for years on end, and at the most impressionable age, withdrawn from the tasks of their time, and estranged. Instead of learning to see things as they were, and freeing themselves from the dangerous tradition of German escape-idealism, they became victims of a deceptive mysticism which made them easy victims for the National Socialists. Furthermore, by yielding to the lure of this mysticism, toward which an attitude of rational criticism was sure to mean angry expulsion from the "group," these boys lost all capacity for criticism. At a time when the blind obedience of the soldier was regarded as unworthy of rational men, they adopted the habit of a far more sinister obedience: the servile subordination of the mind under the yoke of an ideology.

The divine essence, or *élan vital*, or life force, or vril, was believed to be electromagnetic—"Theo-zoological," in Lanz's terminology. Since the sun was the repository of this energy, it became the fashion for German youth groups, as for occult groups generally, to adopt the emblem of the swastika, a symbol for the sun. The festival of the changing sun, an old pagan ritual, was given a new occult twist by the Sera Circle, in that the cosmic rays were thought to emit esoteric knowledge along with warmth. List's Armanen believed that the solar symbol held the key to an ancient "secret science" and that by communing with the ghostly spirits present in certain Germanic ruins, mysterious veils of the past would be lifted. The Cosmic Circle practiced pagan rituals intended to arouse the life force and awaken clairvoyant powers in people of Germanic blood. In their songs and dances, the groups tried to recreate that primordial kinship with nature which they supposed ancient man to have had. They abhorred science and reason as enemies of the life of the soul. Many of them became vegetarians and teetotalers, for they believed that the purification of the physical body would help the soul to see reality. They threw over orthodox medicine for spiritual and herbal healing, which were somehow felt to be closer to the primal source.

The youth movement in Germany was essentially conservative because it stressed the importance of the link with the past—not with the traditions of one's parents and grandparents, but with the rites of one's remote ancestors. While Communist youth was being taught to believe in a classless society in which the individual was subordinated to the state, völkisch youth was being taught that the Aryan individual was bound to the state through his hereditary ties, that peasantry and rulers were one folk and each had his proper place in the hierarchy. The peasantry was rhapsodized over and imitated in dance, song, and dress as being "organic" folk. But like the Communists, völkisch youth held the bourgeoisie to be contemptible—the source of all misery. After World War I, the German youth movements took on more and more the character of anti-Semitic societies, seeing the Jew as the exemplar of the bourgeoisie. Little by little, Jewish youth was excluded from membership in youth organizations.

At the same time that they were practicing spirituality through vegetarianism and abstinence from sex, boys and girls were being encouraged by leaders like de Lagarde, Langbehn, Chamberlain, and Fritsch to extol force, as the Crusaders had done, in a holy war against the enemies: Freemasons, liberals, and Jews.

The politicization of the youth movement came just after World War I, when the paramilitary Free Corps attracted many former members, to pass them on in turn to the Nazi party, and in some cases, the SS. Their education in obedience, discipline, selfless service to an ideal, romanticism, and the occult—in a patriarchy where fathers had been taken away to the war—helped to make the transition easy, and they were eager to follow the Führer wherever he might lead. As one völkisch youth put it:

> One often hears the question why it was that youth spontaneously rallied to Hitler. But the experiences of war, revolution, and inflation

supply an explanation. We were not spared anything. We knew and felt the worries in the house. The shadow of necessity never left our table and made us silent. We were rudely pushed out of our childhood and not shown the right path. The struggle for life got to us early. Misery, shame, hatred, lies, and civil war imprinted themselves on our souls and made us mature early. So we searched, and found Adolf Hitler. What attracted us like a magnet was precisely the fact that he only made demands of us and promised us nothing. He demanded of every person a total commitment to his movement and therefore to Germany.

German youth had always been highly organized. In the Weimar Republic some 4.5 million boys and girls under twenty-one were members of organizations connected with the National Board of German Youth Associations. Under Hitler, the youth movement became a holy crusade. By the end of 1934, the Hitler Youth included 6 million members, ranging in age from ten to eighteen. Membership in other youth organizations was officially discouraged and disintegrated under pressure. Parents and church groups were in jeopardy if they failed actively to support the Hitler Youth, so that eventually all the young in Germany, according to the contemporary observer, Stephen H. Roberts, were "stamped into the same mould" and emerged "as unquestioning automata, physically fit and mentally sponges for the official Hitler hero-worship," with the slogan "Command and we follow . . . the standard is more than death."

The brainwashing actually began in the cradle. Even the fairy tales read to babies instilled the propaganda that the Führer had been sent from heaven to kill the wicked enemy who was eager to devour little children.

The "ideological training" Hitler decreed was "to bring up that unspoilt generation which will consciously find its way back to primitive instinct." Fairy tales were saturated with "struggle" and "race" as "a childhood means of education to a heroic view of the world and of life." One volume was titled *People Fight*. The *Robinson Crusoe* age groups were taught: "From an early age youth must be able to face a time when it may be ordered not merely to act, but also to die . . . [it must] simply learn to think like our ancestors again. A man's greatest honor lies in death before the enemy of his country." Hitler Youth sang: "God is struggle and struggle is our blood, and that is why we were born." A book of tales published for them in 1935 gave them the battle cry: "No one shall live after the Leader's death."

The system of indoctrination was perfect. At ten, each boy joined the

Young Folk; and each girl, the Union of German Maidens. They received uniforms and took a pledge to devote their lives to the Führer. His will was to be their will. Hitler knew well how to accomplish this:

This youth learns nothing else than to think German, to act German, and if these boys enter our organization at the age of 10, . . . then 4 years later they come from the Jungfolk into the Hitler Youth, and we keep them there for another 4 years, and then we certainly don't give them back into the hands of the originators of our old classes and estates, but take them straight into the party, into the Labour Front, the SA or the SS, the NSKK, and so on. And if they are there for another 2 years or a year and a half and still haven't become complete National Socialists, then they go into the Labour Service and are polished for another 6 or 7 months, all with a symbol, the German spade. And any class consciousness or pride of status that may be left here and there is taken over by the Wehrmacht for further treatment for 2 years, and when they come back after 2, 3, or 4 years, we take them straight into the SA, SS, and so on again, so that they shall in no case suffer a relapse, and they don't feel free again as long as they live. And if anyone says to me, yes, but there will always be a few left over: National Socialism is not at the end of its days, but only at the beginning!

The child who was willing to assert himself as a leader in this system no longer had to worry about his future. He knew that he could rise to the top of an elitist cult. His family usually did not object, out of fear, ambition, or ignorance. Many did not realize until too late that a dreadful Pied Piper had taken their children away from them. Hitler himself remarked that it was a "quite special secret pleasure" to see "how the people around us fail to realize what is really happening to them."

Not every child throve under the training program. The more intelligent and individualistic must have found it unbearable to be watched like prisoners. Innocuous conversations were recorded by eavesdroppers. True friendship was impossible, because everyone was afraid to say what they really thought. One Labor Service inmate described what conversation inevitably was:

Camp conversations would begin somewhat in this fashion, when one was fairly sure of being able to trust the other person. "The camp's fine, isn't it?" "Yes, very"—with emphasis on the word "very"—"There's

such a friendly spirit, don't you think, such spontaneous comradeship?''
"Yes, and such excellent leadership, isn't there?" "Yes, I am thankful
to be able to share such a valuable experience and to see eye to eye with
my leaders.''

But most young people succumbed to the brainwashing, even if their
inclinations went counter to Nazi dogma. One young teacher, the daughter
of a liberal professor, joined the Party under pressure:

At first I just made myself do it. The Nazi accounts were so fantastic—
plots of world-Jewry, etc.—that I could hardly keep from laughing as I
read them; but of course I had to be careful. It was somewhat of a shock
to find how readily the children accepted these Nazi fabrications. But the
most amazing thing of all was, that after a few years of going through the
routine, I began to believe the stories myself and could no longer
distinguish in my own mind between propaganda and truth.

Paragraph 2 of the Law Relating to the Hitler Youth read that "all young
Germans in the Reich area are, except in the parental home and at school, to
be physically, mentally and morally reared in the spirit of National Socialism for service to the nation and the national community in the Hitler
Youth.'' For most young people, there was little resistance. The enthusiasm for the Führer canceled out all other interests. Even when church
groups or parents pleaded with children to keep away from the Hitler
Youth, their hearts and souls had been captured by the uniforms, the fife
and drums, and the example of their peers, so that not to be included in the
Führer's glorious movement became the worst kind of punishment.

The generation gap became a battle for the mind in some families, where
parents who opposed the regime found it impossible to express their ideas
to their idolatrous children. Parents rejecting Nazi dogma while their
children shifted loyalty to the family to loyalty to the Party must have
experienced great pain. In many households, one's offspring became one's
worst enemy. It was not at all uncommon for children to denounce their
parents as traitors to the state.

Children worshipped the Führer as a god. To be singled out to see him
and speak to him was to be elevated to demigod. The training fostered this
kind of fanaticism while at the same time discarding intellectual inquiry.
Philosophy was held to be morbid. Universal education was, according to
Hitler, "the most corrosive and disintegrative poison ever devised by

liberalism." Each stratum of society needed to learn what was necessary for its particular purposes, and nothing more. All education was to be under constant surveillance, with the "broad mass of the lowest class" receiving "the blessings of illiteracy."

Hitler was right. His pedagogy *was* hard, not only for German youth but for all mankind. He took the prevailing knowledge about mass propaganda techniques and applied them zealously. Almost every moment in the youth camps was regimented. The mind was led step by step through an intensive drill to accept Nazi principles. The days were long and active, and the political indoctrination was particularly effective when minds were tired. Without physical force, then, youth was brainwashed from the 5:45 A.M. reveille to the 9:30 P.M. lights-out, with lectures on the healthy family, the healthy nation, hereditarily diseased offspring, Germanic civilization, and Lebensraum theories instilled along with a love of heroism, toughness, silence, and loyalty, and above all, a contempt for weakness.

By these tactics, the Nazis created a generation of youth so brutalized that they were capable of roaring with hysterical laughter while watching civilians in occupied countries being executed and, when they ran out of civilians, hanging kittens from miniature gallows. A British soldier, writing home, remarked: "It is not even organized terrorism, but cruelty and bestiality practised for its own sake, the worst offenders being German boys between the ages of 16 and 18." Another observer, a Swiss who lived in Germany in 1943, noticed in these boys "an acquired military rigidity together with a quivering nervousness . . . bright laughter side by side with a desperate seriousness, and a self-assured, grown-up manner alternating with childish and uncontrollable behavior." The boys he was describing were ten to eighteen years old.

The impact of the "hate" training is brought home dramatically when we realize that these young hoods, when captured in the war, refused blood transfusions if they could not be certain of the donor's racial purity, preferring to die instead.

When they were questioned by the Allies about the atrocities, they shrugged off their responsibility: "I saw women and children killed, but did not pay any attention to it; I have no opinion, I obey."

By Nazi standards, their education had been perfect. All morality and intelligence had been propagandized out of them. Before Hitler came, Germany had been one of the most respected countries in the world for its high standard of education. By February 11, 1941, the illiteracy that Hitler prized was an accomplished fact, according to an official press account, which reported: "Apprentices not only seem unable to spell properly, but also fall far below the old standards in arithmetic. At a recent examination for 179 apprentices, 94 spelled names without capital letters, and 81 misspelled Goethe's name [in 17 different ways]. . . ."

After the war, the Allies were worried about how to rehabilitate these morally depraved youngsters. A German teacher provided a solution:

> Why do we conquer such distant foreign lands if, in so doing, we must leave untilled the field of our own children's souls which is close at hand?
>
> Never mind textbooks, the first job will be to teach these youngsters how to love!

Love was something Himmler actually tried to instill in youth, though not in the sense that the teacher meant it. Departing from the puritanism of the earlier youth movement, he urged that the mating of vigorous young males with healthy females was so important to the future of the Aryan race that procreation was no longer a private matter, but a duty to the state. Irresponsible youth was encouraged to produce children out of wedlock, and unwed mothers were elevated to hitherto undreamed-of heights. Although abortions for adult women almost disappeared (in 1940 there were less than a third of what there had been in 1931), abortions for fourteen- and fifteen-year-old girls rose, as did the incidence of pregnancies. Secret reports dealt with homosexuality among Hitler Youth, which officials blamed on the old youth-group past of many members and leaders, when a homoerotic ideal had been fostered.

One of Himmler's major preoccupations was the question of how to produce more male children to make up for those killed in the war. He had heard there was a custom in the Swabian Alps of a man abstaining from alcohol for a whole week, going for a twenty-kilometer walk in the early afternoon, and copulating with his wife on his return. She had done nothing but sleep and eat wholesome food for the week. This was believed to bring about the birth of a male child. Himmler asked an SS doctor to comment, but never got an answer.

Himmler dreamed up Lebensborn, a chain of maternity homes which looked after unwed mothers and provided foster homes for illegitimate babies. He believed the organization would result in several thousand more choice births annually. Every SS officer had to join it and support it with his dues, 5 to 8 percent of his salary. Other SS men were not forced to become members. Himmler believed that "Nietzsche's Superman could be attained by means of breeding" and warned his men that "without multiplying our blood we shall not be able to maintain the Great Germanic Empire that is in the process of coming into existence." He encouraged his "valuable and racially pure men" to become "conception assistants" and overcome their bourgeois qualms about fathering children out of wedlock. Lebensborn, he said, was "a unique phenomenon and can be the basis for a new advance of the Germanic race."

He tried to create the impression that he was learned in genetics. Citing "the marvelous authority of German folklore," he theorized that when conception took place in a Nordic cemetery, babies inherited the spirit of "all the dead heroes who lay therein." Lists of such cemeteries were published regularly in the SS periodical *Das Schwarze Korps*. One English wag, on learning of this, punned: "One might say that these lists give a new ring to the phrase 'poking about in graveyards.' "

Himmler must have been disappointed with the total output of "new beings" at Lebensborn. In 1938, two years after the program officially started, the seven Lebensborn homes accepted only 653 mothers, 40 percent of the applicants who had applied. Racial requirements were so exacting that the majority were turned away. In 1939, however, there were homes in Steinhöring, Polzin, Klosterheide (Mark), Hohehörst, and in the Vienna woods. Later, more hospitals, children's homes, and sanitoria were added from former Jewish properties. Directing offices were set up in Bromberg, as well as in Belgium and Holland. But, for all that, after nine operational years, the official figures for births at Lebensborn were recorded as 12,000, of which half were illegitimate.

Louis Hagen, in *Follow My Leader*, reports one Lebensborn mother as saying:

At the Tegernsee hostel, I waited until the tenth day after the beginning of my period and was medically examined; then I slept with an SS man who had also to perform his duty with another girl. When pregnancy was diagnosed, I had the choice of returning home or going straight into a maternity home. . . . The birth was not easy, but no good German woman would think of having artificial injections to deaden the pain.

Girls considered it an honor to be chosen. One maiden announced proudly to fellow passengers on a train: "I am going to the SS *Ordensburg* in Sonthofen to have myself impregnated.'' Naturally, young girls in the Hitler Youth were encouraged to try motherhood. Rewards were exemption from Labor Service and financial bonuses.

One Labor Service internee wrote to her fiancé:

> The first question they ask a Labor Service girl is, who's going to have a baby for the Führer? Then the girls go into a camp and have to stay there for a year. First be used by SS men, then stay for a year and have a child. If you do all right they slip you RM [reichsmarks] 1,000 and let you go. . . .

The leaders of the camps gave their blessings to these liaisons. One wrote to the mother of a pregnant girl, to bring the glad tidings that she was soon to "present the Führer with a child." If parents did not particularly care for this manner of bestowing gifts, there was nothing they could do. As one Labor Service inmate cautioned her family: "You better not beat me if I come home with a baby, or I'll denounce you!"

To get the right kind of offspring, Himmler even ordered the kidnapping of racially pure children from occupied countries.

Thus, the methodical indoctrination of a whole nation with a conglomeration of irrational ideas—mystical, occult, racist, and anti-human—led to the robotization of the German people, particularly the young, who were most susceptible. As J. G. Siebert, in *The Remaking of German Youth*, remarks:

> The reason why German youth allowed itself to be tricked lies in the fact that it had itself submitted to self-escapement, irrationalism and mysticism, that it had willingly given away its rational powers and its will to independent action. It had given up mastery over itself, and when the Nazis fell upon it with their demagogery, it became an easy victim.

In a relatively short time, the good effects of civilization had been bred out of them, and they had shown themselves capable of performing the most atrocious deeds without any pangs of conscience.

CHAPTER 12

Prophets of the Third Reich

Awareness of one's national heritage and blood ties with the
Aryan race are indivisibly bound up with astrological
science.

—German astrological magazine

Astrology is one aspect of the occult tradition with which the Nazis have
been openly identified. It is an important part of that tradition. According
to astrological theory, the harmony of nature expressed in the planetary
movements is the same as that expressed in individual personalities and
societies. Therefore, the past, present and future can be interpreted by
certain cyclic and numerical calculations of heavenly bodies. If, the occultist argues, the human temperature is lower in the morning, why may we
not observe distinct differences between different periods, people, and
races, since they, too, follow certain periodicities?

Occultists are particularly fond of the law of correspondences, exemplified by the saying attributed to Hermes Trismegistus: "As above, so
below." They see a reciprocal relationship between the microcosm and the
macrocosm, the stars providing a language by which life can be read, a
symbolic master-plan of the hierarchical cosmos; and one of the purposes
of the occult, as they perceive it, is to give men the wisdom to free
themselves from bondage to the fortune in their stars. Through special
knowledge, they believe they can develop the psychic powers to influence

events. To understand astrology is to be able to use a kind of mental alchemy by which the negative aspects of life can be transmuted into good—if one is properly initiated, of course.

From the late nineteenth century on, the Germans were eager to use astrology in their daily lives. They had been particularly impressed with Franz Anton Mesmer's attempts to place astrology on a scientific footing. An Austrian who had studied medicine in Vienna, he applied his theory of animal magnetism to heavenly bodies in his first book, *De Influxu Planetarum in Corpus Humanum* ("Of the Influence of the Planets on the Human Body"). The universe he described was held together by an "aetheric continuum," of which the stars and planets were a constituent part, and from which flowed "animal magnetism." Illness was simply failure to draw effectively on one's aetheric continuum reserves, and Mesmer's apparatus was designed to help people tap this source—this intangible universal force which pervaded space and exercised a hidden influence on human affairs.

Mesmer learned of the researches of Empress Maria Theresa's court astrologer, who enjoyed amazing luck in treating the ill on the basis of Paracelsus' theory of correspondences, or sympathies. What the court astrologer did was to apply magnets to the affected part of the patient's body. Mesmer broadened this theory.

Animal magnetism was more widely practiced by doctors in Germany than anywhere else in Europe, as the eminent turn-of-the-century British clergyman, Frank Podmore, observed in his book, *From Mesmer to Christian Science*. There was no centralized medical academy to impose its rules on the "profession." Mesmerism was studied in German universities. Court physicians and medical professors wrote learned treatises on it. Experiments were repeated endlessly. Podmore reported: "The magnetic fluid could be seen radiating as a stream of light from the eyes and the fingers of the operator and the poles of a magnet, from the heart of a living frog or the spinal marrow of a newly killed ox."

German magnetists threw themselves enthusiastically into clairvoyance and somnambulism. Since the animal fluid could magnetize over space, many instances of extrasensory communications were noted. According to Podmore:

> Clairvoyance at a distance was apparently much commoner in Germany and northern Europe generally at this time than in France. The cases quoted are rarely, however, recorded with sufficient detail to serve

any purpose other than that of attesting the prevalence of the belief, and some of the instances are strongly suggestive of collusion.

The special contribution of the German nation, however, to the early history of Animal Magnetism consists of the revelations concerning the spiritual world dictated by several somnambules in the state of ecstasy.

Such interests flourish in cataclysmic times and are exploited by adventurers like Madame Blavatsky. Inspired by her challenge to Darwinism, other occult leaders copied her peculiar package, so satisfying to educated people who were not prepared to gainsay the findings of science, yet were not prepared to give up the mysteries of religion, either. Scientific theory was not so well understood by the layman that it could hold its own against Madame Blavatsky's fanciful ramblings. In her variation of the Eastern doctrine of human cycles, she read the Atlantean zodiacal record and predicted the end of certain races whose "time was up."

Men like Lanz von Liebenfels, Guido von List, and the master astrologer, Rudolf von Sebottendorff, elaborated on this, and German astrology became intimately bound up with racism. Its ideologists borrowed heavily from Madame Blavatsky to show that the ancient Germans had been keepers of a secret science which had been wiped out by Judeo-Christianity. Lanz and Sebottendorff read in the movement of the planets the coming of a divine Führer who would establish a racist regime. List, in his book, *Die Religion der Ario-Germanen in ihrer Esoterik und Exoterik* ("The Religion of the Aryan Germans in Its Esoteric and Exoteric Aspects"), revealed the "secret" that the moon was the forefather of the human race, and the swastika "one of the holiest secret signs." List believed that the mystery of the heavens would be revealed by departed spirits, in an extrasensory way.

The effect of World War I was to intensify German interest in animal magnetism, Theosophy, and astrology. Inflation drove some to suicide and others to the "sure" knowledge contained in horoscopes. The German astrologer Wilhelm Wulff reports in his book, *Zodiac and Swastika*:

. . . by the November Revolution of 1918, inflation was making headway, well-established businesses were crashing, and suicides were a daily event. In this period of tremendous economic and political uncertainty, hypnosis, mesmerism, clairvoyance, and every form of occultism flourished. Such interests are promoted by catastrophic situations. In post-war Germany, hypnotists, clairvoyants and mind readers were suddenly able to fill huge concert halls. There was scarcely a single large music hall or cabaret that did not stage a telepathic act. Enormous placards and newspaper advertisements pompously proclaimed: "The Most Important Parapsychologist," "The Woman with a Thousand Eyes" (Madame Karoli at the Busch Circus), "The Great Enigma, an Outstanding Achievement in the Sphere of Occult Science, the Lady Who Tells You All," etc. Swindle or not, both public and press found it all fascinating. I was very soon revolted by this fairground occultism. . . .

Konrad Heiden adds this personal observation of the same period:

The churches raged. . . . But if one had accused these astrologers, quacks, necromancers, and fake radiologists of witchcraft and sorcery, most of them would have replied indignantly that they occupied themselves with science—naturally, a science that the "experts" did not understand, for it was the science of the future, perhaps a science predicated on experiments that were still imperfect. . . .
. . . there was much talk of intuition, of presentiment, of what they called "vision" and the like. But nearly always it was considered an "advance" by abnormally endowed natures into certain fields of the spirit that in the near future would be investigated by conventional methods. The stock explanation in that world of deception and self-deception was that everything was done "along strictly scientific lines," which shows to what extent the cult of science had taken the place of religion. . . .

One magus, Erik Jan Hanussen, who received notoriety as the "Prophet of the Third Reich" and the "Magician of Berlin," was credited with having taught Hitler all that he knew about mass psychology, which was considerable. Walter Langer, a psychiatrist, wrote in his secret report to the Allies:

According to Strasser, during the early 1920's Hitler took regular lessons in speaking and in mass psychology from a man named Hanussen, who was also a practicing astrologer and fortuneteller. He was an extremely clever individual who taught Hitler a great deal concerning the importance of staging meetings to obtain the greatest dramatic effect. . . . It is possible that Hanussen had some contact with a group

of astrologers, referred to by von Wiegand, who were very active in
Munich at this time. Through Hanussen Hitler, too, may have come in
contact with this group, for von Wiegand writes: "When I first knew
Adolf Hitler in Munich, in '21 and '22, he was in touch with a circle that
believed firmly in the portents of the stars. There was much whispering
of the coming of 'another Charlemagne and a new Reich.' "

Born Herschel Steinschneider in Vienna in 1889, Hanussen pretended to
descent from a long line of Danish noblemen, although his father actually
was a small-time itinerant Jewish vaudevillian. The son followed in the
dancing footsteps of the father and joined a traveling show at twelve, as
trapeze artist, lion tamer, stable boy, and folk singer. And these roles did
not begin to exhaust his versatility. In Istanbul, without resources, he
created an *ersatz* Franz Lehar operetta. On his way back to Vienna, to
freeload aboard ship, he impersonated a singer and agreed to work his way
home, but a scratchy throat prevented singing. Once home, he blackmailed
people to keep their names out of a paper he edited, and made money from
others by giving them free publicity.

By this time he had changed his name to Erik Jan Hanussen and had
Before World War I, he discovered the world of magic illusion, and in
the army he set himself up as a clairvoyant, with considerable help from
someone in the army post office. Whether or not he believed he really
possessed extrasensory perception, he became a masterful hypnotist. He
also learned how to dowse for water, and wrote a book for other magicians
who wanted to put on mind-reading acts: *The Road to Telepathy: Explanation and Practice*. After the war, he wrote another, *Thought Reading: A
Primer for Telepathy*, in which he gave invaluable advice to the neophyte
magician: "The illusion of the supernatural must surround him in the eyes
of his audience, which will be a thousand times more manageable when it
has become a group of believers. With success, self-confidence rises, and
with self-confidence the power of persuasion itself."

By this time he had changed his name to Erik Jan Hanussen and had
created his own reputation for clairvoyance and other supernatural powers,
despite his confession: "If I were to strip away all that is mystical or
supernatural, if I were to show thought reading for what it is, we would
arrive at virtuosity in the knowledge of audience psychology, linked to the
meticulous study of procedures concerning ideomotor motions [based on
ideas rather than on reflexes]." Here, finally, was a man who employed the
scientific method. Others less candid had paved the way for him. There is a
natural affinity between magic tricks and fakirism which believers had no

will to discover. Many "masters of wisdom" were also accomplished magicians. Madame Blavatsky had been, and when she was discovered at her tricks, her disciples protested that this was what the public had driven her to. As magicians, from Houdini in the twenties to Milbourne Christopher and Randi in our own time, have demonstrated, most, if not all, feats of clairvoyance can be duplicated by the magician, and a look at a catalog of magicians' equipment bears them out. The magicians, of course, resent the mediums, because they feel the mediums are using the same tricks they do (and, in fact, they have caught many of the most famous mediums in the act, so to speak). The stage magicians are using their skills and techniques to provide honest entertainment, and feel that the mediums, psychics, and faith healers are using those skills to gull, cheat, and sell false dreams and false hopes.

In 1931, Hanussen met Hitler, joined the Nazi party, raised the swastika flag on his car, and befriended leading Nazi officials. Hitler knew the value of using men with Hanussen's gifts to publicize his image as a man of historic destiny. Hanussen put himself at the service of the Nazi cause in astrological forecasts published by his swastika-trimmed paper. He also sought to put the Party in his debt by lending large sums to the SA leader of Berlin, Count Wolf Heinrich Helldorf, an opportunist as impressive as Hanussen himself. Prominent Nazis attended fashionable séances which Hanussen staged at his Palace of Occultism and were pleased to listen to his cheerful prognostications for the Party. One that was not so cheerful will cause him to be remembered whenever the controversial Reichstag fire comes up.

In February 1933, soon after Hitler was named chancellor, Hanussen opened the Palace of Occultism to actors, actresses, and important members of the Party. At a midnight séance, in an atmosphere of garish splendor embellished with gilded zodiac symbols and bugged with secret microphones to pry out intimate details from an unsuspecting audience (a common showman's trick which the Nazis were to use again in the fashionable brothel they instituted for important officials, German and foreign), Hanussen went into his trance:

I see a vast and distinguished room. . . . Portraits of prominent men of history hang on the walls. They are men who have led Germany through much agony. Are they not the chancellors of the Reich? Yes, this is the Conference Room of the Chancellery. Noise penetrates through the windows. The Storm Troopers move down the Wilhelmstrasse. There has been a magnificent victory. The people want Hitler. Victory, Victory! Hitler is victorious. Resistance is useless. But the noise comes closer. Is there a struggle? Shooting? No . . . no . . . it is not that. . . . I see flames, enormous flames. . . . It is a terrible conflagration that has broken out. Criminals have set the fire.

They want to hurl Germany into last-minute chaos, to nullify the victory. They are setting fire to a large public building. One must crush this vermin. They want to resist Hitler's victory. Only the mailed fist of an awakened Germany can hold back chaos and the threat of civil war. . . .

The following evening, the Reichstag was in flames. The question as to who started the fire has not been resolved to this day. The suspicion that the Nazis themselves were implicated is strengthened by the fact that Berlin police president Helldorf went directly to bed after hearing of the fire. It was still raging when the police arrested a Dutch Communist who was found on the premises. The Nazis linked him with a Communist plot which they failed to make stick, but the Dutchman was executed. Some people claim that Hanussen had hypnotized him into starting the fire. Hanussen had pledged himself, after all,

to be the first, if necessary, to devote everything I own and am, when the time comes, to make a sacrifice at the altar of Germany. I have encountered the readiness for sacrifice among all those who stood behind the banner of the National Concept; I know that Adolf Hitler sacrificed his all for this national idea; I saw Storm Trooper veterans in torn shoes and in thin jackets standing in the icy winds for hours to perform their duty; I have observed selflessness, integrity, and true patriotism among the millions who back Hitler. . . . and so I had no choice but to demonstrate my respect and gratitude, unhesitatingly, in spite of everything, to serve the truth.

Whether or not Hanussen had advance notice of the fire, he probably assumed his prediction of it would assure his stature as a prophet. It did not. Six weeks later, he was snatched from the entrance to his theater by Helldorf's orders, and murdered in the woods near Berlin. Helldorf, perpetually bankrupt, had borrowed money from Hanussen, but whether this was the motivation for the murder, or whether it related to Hanussen's knowledge about the fire, is still a mystery. The fire augured well for the

Nazis, on the other hand. It enabled them to do away altogether with the need for free elections, under the guise of preventing an imminent Communist takeover.

Once firmly entrenched, the Nazis continued to call upon the services of soothsayers, even though official policy was to harass and banish them. The astrologer Gerda Walther, in an article in *Tomorrow* entitled "Hitler's Black Magicians," observed a "complete lack of unity" regarding occultism. "Not only is there an absence of 'coordination,' but often there are different and even opposing points of view."

As soon as Hitler came into the public eye, he was the target for astrological prognostications. But after 1933, an astrologer tempted fate if he cast the Führer's horoscope, and none were so bold as to dare. Fearing unfavorable predictions, Hitler decreed that police regulations equate astrology with fortunetelling, and Paragraph 2 read:

> For purposes of these police regulations fortune-telling is understood as a prediction of future events, the divination of the present or the past, and all other forms of revelation not based on natural processes of perception. It specifically includes the reading of cards, the casting of horoscopes, the explanation of the stars, and the interpretation of omens and dreams.

As Himmler later confessed to Wilhelm Wulff, the reason for the strictures against astrologers was that if they were not Nazis, they might see their calling as universally applicable to all humans, whether they were Negroes, Indians, Chinese, or Aryans, "in crass opposition" to the Nazi concept of the racial soul. "No one doctrine," argued Himmler, "can cover all cases." But he left no doubt in Wulff's mind that he was committed to a belief in astrology and related occult studies:

> He told me about a few of his own experiences and observations at certain phases of the moon. His ancestors, he said, had been familiar with peasant lore, calculating the right time to plant crops. . . . He . . . began projects at certain, but not generally known, phases of the moon. . . .

He was fond of citing the important place of astrologers and fortunetellers in the court of Frederick the Great.

A friend of Wulff's, Ellic Howe, who was employed by the British

Secret Service in World War II, discovered, by reading astrological studies
in Gestapo files after the war, that Himmler was in good company. Wulff
repeats his assertion that "German astrology was supreme in the 1930's"
and it engaged the attention of other important Nazis, like Walter Schellenberg and Rudolf Hess. It was largely thanks to Hess that the so-called
"witchcraft act" of 1934 against astrologers and occultists was circum-
vented. When a former planetarium director on Alfred Rosenberg's staff in
the Department for the Promotion of German Writing made an official
declaration that astrology should be banned, Hess disagreed, on the
grounds that there might be something to it. It was this bias, some believe,
which caused Hess to make the mysterious flight to Scotland. Howe reports
in his book, *Astrology: A Recent History Including the Untold Story of Its
Role in World War II*, that a confidant revealed to him:

> Hess's astrological foible strengthened his own conviction that every-
> thing possible must be done and hazarded in order to end hostilities
> without delay, because at the end of April and beginning of May 1941
> Hitler's astrological aspects were unusually malefic. Hess interpreted
> these aspects to mean that he, personally, must take the dangers that
> threatened the *Führer* upon his shoulders in order to save Hitler and
> restore peace in Germany. Time and again Hess's astrological "ad-
> visor" had told him that Anglo-German relations were threatened by a
> deep-seated crisis of confidence. . . . Indeed, at this time there were
> very dangerous [planetary] oppositions in Hitler's horoscope.

Hitler, although he publicly ridiculed the occult tastes of his disciples,
was equally superstitious; and his chief architect and later minister of
armaments and war production, Albert Speer, related that he himself
witnessed a number of instances of this, such as the occasion when

> Hitler had solemnly laid the cornerstone for the House of German Art in
> Munich. He delivered the ceremonial hammer blows with a fine silver
> hammer Troost had designed especially for this day. But the hammer
> broke. [Troost died three months later and] Hitler remarked to us:
> "When the hammer shattered I knew at once it was an evil omen.
> Something is going to happen, I thought. Now we know why the
> hammer broke. The architect was destined to die."

Hermann Rauschning, a leader of the Danzig Senate who fled Germany
in 1940, also attests to Hitler's occult leanings. In *The Voice of Destruction*, he writes:

One day when Hitler seemed in an approachable mood, a far-sighted woman in his circle said to him warningly:

"My Führer, don't touch black magic. As yet both white and black are open to you. But once you have embarked upon black magic it will dominate your destiny. It will hold you captive. Don't choose the quick and easy successes. There lies before you the power over a realm of pure spirits. Do not allow yourself to be led away from your true path by earthbound spirits, which will rob you of creative power."

Hitler was fond at times of this sort of mystical talk. Only in such guise could any serious warning be offered to him. This woman friend expressed in her way what everyone who came in touch with Hitler was bound to feel: Hitler was abandoning himself to forces which were carrying him away—forces of dark and destructive violence. He imagined that he still had freedom of choice, but he had long been in bondage to a magic which might well have been described, not only in metaphor but in literal fact, as that of evil spirits. And instead of a man emerging step by step from the obscurity of his youth, and freeing himself from its dross in his upward course, we witnessed the development of a man possessed, the helpless prey of the powers of darkness.

Black magic, white magic—Hitler is the typical person with no firm foundation, with all the shortcomings of the superficial, of the man without reverence, quick to judge and quick to condemn. He is one of those with no spiritual tradition, who, being caught by the first substitute for it that they meet, hold tenaciously to that, lest they fall back into Nothingness. He belongs also to the type of German who is starving for the unattainable. For all those who have been unsuccessful in the battle of life National Socialism is the great worker of magic. And Hitler himself is the first of these; thus he has become the master-enchanter and the high priest of the religious mysteries of Nazidom.

Hitler's henchmen make more and more play with this quality of his of supreme magician. . . .

After Hitler's rise, someone in Himmler's department was given an astrological forecast by a Swiss friend, Karl Ernst Krafft, an astrologer with a predilection for the same sort of theories about the "spirit of language" and "word magic" which distinguished Guido von List. Krafft was well versed in Latin, Greek, German, French, Italian, Spanish, Dutch, and English. He had used his astrological talents to forecast trends on the commodities market. Around 1938, he was living in the Black Forest with two women who were interested in Rudolf Steiner. Hitler appealed to Krafft as "the conqueror of the mechanistic way of life."

Krafft predicted to his friend that Hitler's life would hang in the balance between November 7 and 10, 1939. During that time, Hitler attended an anniversary celebration of the 1923 *Putsch* in the Munich Hofbrauhaus. He left just before a bomb went off and tore apart the beer cellar. Krafft zealously wired Hess, thrusting his prediction under his nose, and adding that the stars still indicated that Hitler would not be safe for a few more days. Krafft was promptly arrested.

Himmler, meanwhile, was working on tracking down the failed assassin by interviewing a Viennese trance medium who had been ordered to his office.

Goebbels, as propaganda minister, had more practical concerns. He just happened, at that particular time, to have developed an interest in Nostradamus, the sixteenth-century French prophet, not for his verse quatrains, but for his propaganda possibilities. He must have been delighted to find in Krafft a man who was not only familiar with Nostradamus' obscure verses but who actually believed that Germany's triumph over the Allies—and over future enemies, as well—could be deciphered from them.

Krafft came to work for the propaganda ministry and began using his special knowledge of Nostradamus as a means of psychological warfare. Nostradamus had been deliberately obscure, to keep his secrets from being understood by any but the initiated. The infinite permutations of possible interpretations had made his quatrains popular propaganda devices for centuries. Thus Krafft had an embarrassment of riches from which to choose so as to interpret Germany's victory. Quatrain III-76 presumably predicted the birth of National Socialism:

> In Germany will be born diverse sects,
> approaching very near happy paganism.
> The heart captive and receipts small;
> they will return to paying the true tithe.

Krafft was in deadly earnest when he interpreted a passage like the following to mean great discomfort for Great Britain:

> In the islands shall be so horrid tumults,
> That nothing shall be heard but a warlike surprise,

So great shall be the insult of the robbers,
That everyone shall shelter himself under the great look.

Goebbels' diary entry for November 22, 1939, reads: "This is a thing
we can exploit for a long time. I forbid all printing of these forecasts by
Monsieur Nostradamus. They must be disseminated only by handbills,
hand-written, or at most typed, secretly, and in the manner of snowball
letters. The thing must have an air of being forbidden. . . . Naturally, all
this silly rubbish must also go out to France. . . ."

Pamphlets of Krafft's interpretations were sent in advance of the military
through occupied France and were highly successful in getting their message across. Krafft's exegeses were translated into many different languages, and the output was enormous. They were even "surreptitiously
stuck into people's pockets as they left the movies—as far away as in
Iran!" according to Gerda Walther.

Romania's minister to London, an anti-Nazi awed by Krafft's seemingly
prophetic gifts, wrote him to renew an old acquaintance and to ask for his
astrological predictions about the war. Krafft showed the letter to his Nazi
superiors, and they drafted an answer predicting Germany's victory. When
the Romanian minister received it, he assumed that Krafft must be advising
Hitler, and got the idea of convincing the British to hire the best astrologer
they could find and have him try to second-guess Krafft. If the British could
get their astrologer to find out how Krafft was arriving at the sources for his
advice, they could, first of all, know what Hitler was thinking, and
secondly, influence his thought by preparing forecasts similar to Krafft's
but pro-Allies, and slipping them into Hitler's hands. For the purpose,
Ludwig von Wohl was hired.

A Roman-Catholic Hungarian author of religious books who left Berlin
for London in 1935, he had a reputation among believers in astrology for
his accurate horoscopes of Hitler, Mussolini, Churchill, Chamberlain, and
other prominent people. One of Hitler, in particular, cast in 1931, brought
him to the attention of the international set. Just before the beginning of
World War II, at a Spanish embassy dinner party, he entertained the British
secretary of foreign affairs, Lord Halifax, with astrological predictions,
and was assured that he would have a job if war broke out when he said
it would and if Hitler's invasion of Poland was as rapid as he predicted.

The war was three days early. Ludwig von Wohl became a British
citizen, changed his name to Louis de Wohl, and joined the British army.

In August 1940 an employee of the War Office came to him and asked:
"How would you like to work on a highly secret assignment?"
He liked it very much. Made a captain, paid in cash, and set up in a suite
at Grosvenor House, he worked on his unique task. British Intelligence
believed that Hitler was being advised not only by Krafft but by four other
astrologers, and that he never made a military move without their advice.
Churchill was agreeable to the idea of trying to intercept what Hitler was
being told every day. "Why not try it?" he said. "It could be fun." In
allowing the bizarre appointment, Churchill was assumed to be indulging
one of his mischievous caprices. "After all," he is reported to have said,
"why should Hitler have a monopoly on astrologers?" One commentator
remarked that he may also have "relished the idea of subjecting some
stuffy high-powered official to an astrologer's scrutiny."

Since De Wohl knew all five astrologers who were supposedly advising
Hitler, had worked for some time with Krafft, and was familiar with his
formula, he could guess what he presumed they were telling Hitler. In his
first memo to the British War Office in the beginning of September 1940 he
advised that the Germans would not invade England, because he was sure
that Hitler's astrologers were counseling him against it.

One of De Wohl's tasks was to put out a bogus copy of an astrological
magazine called *Der Zenit*, which looked exactly like the genuine article.
It was intercepted by the Nazis; and Wulff relates that he told Himmler's
assistant, Walter Schellenberg, "that from an astrological point of view it
was a first-class production and indicated that it was the work of experts.
Some very skillful bits of propaganda had been casually inserted in an
otherwise apparently innocuous text. We deduced that this fake had been
manufactured in England."

Wulff was consulted several times by Himmler during 1944 and 1945,
particularly as defeat seemed imminent. Wilhelm Hoetl, who joined the
German Secret Service in 1938, says of Himmler: "His predilection for the
occult sciences also went far beyond the confines of a harmless hobby; it
can with truth be said that all his major decisions hung upon the advice
given to him by his clairvoyant. . . ." According to Hoetl, Schellenberg,
anxious to end the war, had Wulff draw up a horoscope "which would give
Himmler the necessary courage and convince him that he was destined by
Fate to become the Führer and the saviour of the German people. . . ."

Not only Himmler, but the German people pinned their hopes on
astrology. Speer relates that they had

long since stopped believing the newspapers. There was one exception: During the closing months of the war growing bands of desperate people began pinning their hopes on the astrological sheets. Since these were dependent on the Propaganda Ministry, for a variety of reasons they were, as I learned from [Hans] Fritzsche at Nuremberg, used as a tool for influencing public opinion. Fake horoscopes spoke of valleys of darkness which had to be passed through, foretold imminent surprises, intimated happy outcomes. Only in the astrological sheets did the regime still have a future.

In 1945, the day after President Franklin D. Roosevelt died, Goebbels, who may have been a victim of his own propaganda, ordered champagne and phoned Hitler: "My Führer, I congratulate you! Roosevelt is dead. It is written in the stars that the second half of April will be the turning-point for us. This is Friday 13 April. It is the turning-point."

Later, in Hitler's bunker, Goebbels sent for the horoscopes which had been cast for the Führer and for Germany on his accession to the chancellery. They had been given to Himmler for safekeeping. Both predicted the entire outcome of the war: the beginning, in 1939; victory until 1941; then defeat until the second half of April 1945, when there would be a reversal of fortune. Peace would not come until August.

Goebbels, who may have been humoring Hitler, drew historical analogies between the death of Roosevelt and the death of the tsarina during the Seven Years' War with Russia, when Frederick the Great appeared to be defeated until the death turned things around.

But in the end, all the prophets failed them, and the Nazis learned that they could not be saved by the stars.

CHAPTER 13

Jung and the Aryan Unconscious

Even Jung's much-debated interpretation of what was happening in Hitler's Germany in the thirties was not without
insight, though his conduct justifies the suspicion that he
himself, like all too many equally intelligent contemporaries
in Europe, had momentarily turned to the same demonic
powers for salvation and let himself be carried away by them.

—Lewis Mumford, "The Revolt of the Demons,"
The New Yorker, May 23, 1964

It has always been a mystery why intelligent people outside of Germany
in the twenties and thirties were attracted by the Nazi movement. Before
the atrocity stories began to leak out, the Nazis were *persona grata* with a
certain type of mystical temperament which saw in the romantic aspects of
their ideology a refreshing return to "thinking with the blood," as D. H.
Lawrence called it.

The psychologist Carl Jung is a case in point. His interest in the occult
ran very deep, and began very early. In his autobiography, *Memories,
Dreams and Reflections*, he told of his initiation, in dreams of childhood,
to "the secrets of the earth" and "the realm of darkness," "overpowered
by a vision of the whole cosmos," where "lived the 'Other,' who knew

God as a hidden, personal, and at the same time suprapersonal secret. Here nothing separated man from God; indeed, it was as though a human mind looked down upon Creation simultaneously with God."

The young Carl soon discovered that his jolly housewife mother harbored a submerged self, "archaic and ruthless," just as sacred as God, which he later identified with the ancient Germanic realm of Wotan. Sometimes the child would find her doing chores with a strange look in her eyes, muttering incomprehensibly to herself. When he listened more attentively, it was clear that the words were designed for him, and their appropriateness reached "to the very core" of his being.

Her diary recorded experiences with precognition, ghosts, and supranormal phenomena. As a child, her services had often been called upon to protect her theologian father from spectral presences:

> She had to sit behind him when he was writing his sermons, because he could not bear "spirits" passing behind his back and disturbing him. Every week, at a fixed hour, he used to hold intimate conversations with his deceased first wife, very much to the chagrin of the second! Jung's psychiatric diagnosis was that he suffered from "waking hallucinations," though at the same time he dismissed this as a "mere word." [His] second wife, . . . Jung's maternal grandmother, was gifted with "second sight" and could also see "spirits." The family traced this back to an episode when, as a young girl, she lay for thirty-six hours in a state of catalepsy resembling death. Her gifts, however, could stand the test of a more rigorous judgment: she sometimes saw apparitions of persons unknown to her, but whose historical existence was later proved.

Carl was both scared and thrilled by the sense of the uncanny. As a teen-aged student at the *Gymnasium* in Basel, he found a philosophical basis for it in the work of Pythagoras. By this time, the private, secret world which he had learned to inhabit as an escape from his all-powerful mother was much pleasanter than the bourgeois school world from which he was excluded by poverty, provincialism, and personal unpopularity. He saved his ego by retreating into ritual, fantasy, and nature-mysticism. The greatest fantasy, which came unbidden, and which would have earned him the applause of Jonathan Swift and Rabelais, was a masterpiece of unconscious wit in such a stolid fellow: God, from on high, sent down his own personal blast of excrement, appropriately monumental, to bomb the newly decorated roof of the Basel Cathedral.

Jung was convinced that he had been chosen by God for a prophetic mission to herald the dawning Age of Aquarius. At the same time, he felt privy to ancient dark mysteries, which he was not about to reveal, wanting to avoid the fate of Nietzsche, who went mad. Jung had a sense of himself as two distinct personalities, the schoolboy and the wise old man. The schoolboy was himself as he appeared to others. The wise old man was a powerful figure of the Enlightenment, and the young boy owed to this odd presence his sense of being selected for a great work and of being perfectly at home with eighteenth-century ideas and artifacts. The psychologist, looking back at this dichotomy in his youth, insisted that it did not represent a diseased disunion. A recurring daydream, which he was later able to play out in reality, had him ensconced in a medieval castle where, as judge, he ruled over the town. What gave him the power to rule was that, hidden in the tower,

was a thick copper column whose top, branching into a network of tiny capillaries, drew from the air an ineffable spiritual substance which, condensed and transformed by its passage through the metallic column, would reappear at the bottom as finished gold coins. In his gold-making fantasy, Carl, unlike the medieval alchemists, did not use lead or other base metals for raw material, but something "spiritual" diffused in the air. With his hunger for omens, he was bound to retrospectively view this adolescent daydream as presaging his long-lasting fascination with alchemy in later years. A person of less exalted turn of mind might read the same fantasy as pointing to Jung's future adroitness in extracting money from "spirituality."

As outsider and as pagan, he felt much closer to the animal and vegetable kingdoms than to the kingdom of man. Nature was suffused with "numinousness," a term which he came to love and use a great deal. It well described his family's extrasensory experiences.

As it came time, however, to decide on a profession, he was governed by more practical concerns. He did not care to repeat his clergyman father's history of poverty, and in 1895 enrolled as a medical student at the University of Basel. There he was attracted by spiritualists like Johann Zoellner and Emanuel Swedenborg, discussing their theories by the hour. He was far from being alone in his fascination with spiritualism. A number of respectable scientists believed in the existence of occult phenomena and were investigating them. Jung arranged mediumistic séances. In his autobiography, he described how a medium, his fifteen-year-old cousin, made a sturdy antique table and a knife in a drawer break apart. (The family saved the fragmented pieces of knife.) This medium became the subject for Jung's doctoral dissertation, "The Psychology and Pathology of Supposed Occult Phenomena." In it, he talked about the relation of the unconscious to the conscious mind and referred to Sigmund Freud's new theory of hysterical identification. Jung made up his mind to become a psychiatrist and unite his interest in the soul with his interest in medicine.

He did not meet Freud in the flesh until 1907. By then, strong anti-Semitic sentiments were already skulking through Western Europe. Freud was a pariah, both as Jew and as proponent of a controversial theory of sexuality, a subject shrouded with taboo—one Freud himself referred to as "that troublesome factor so unwelcome in good society." It took courage on Jung's part to join the Freudian camp. Then almost thirty-two, Jung had a good deal to lose by associating himself with the Austrian Jew. Also, by becoming Freud's favorite son, he incurred the enmity of older and longer-standing disciples.

Despite mutual respect and admiration, there were insurmountable differences between Jung and Freud. The older man could not share the younger's passion for occultism. When Jung came to visit Freud in Vienna, they discussed precognition and parapsychology in Freud's study. Freud dismissed the matter as "nonsensical," and there came a loud cracking sound from his bookcase. Jung predicted that there would be another in a moment, and interpreted the noise as evidence of the paranormal. Returning home, he wrote Freud that the visit, "most happily, freed me inwardly from the oppressive sense of your paternal authority." Freud replied that the "poltergeist business" left him incredulous. Since Jung's visit, he had heard the sounds from the bookcase repeatedly—not, he hastened to add, when he was thinking of Jung—but he warned his "dear son to keep a cool head, for it is better not to understand something than make such great sacrifices to understanding." Jung's "investigations of the spook complex" Freud took to be "a charming delusion" which he could not share.

Years later, in his autobiography, Jung confessed that, as Freud was disparaging parapsychology, he himself felt "a curious sensation" in his diaphragm, as if it "were made of iron and were becoming red-hot—a glowing vault." Hearing the noise from the bookcase, he feared it would topple over on them. Freud's retort that this was "sheer bosh" made Jung believe that his mentor mistrusted him, and though they never talked about the incident after the exchange of letters, the schism between them grew. Nonetheless, Freud did push for Jung to be elected president of the International Psychoanalytic Association, to the horror of other disciples.

Jung devoted more and more of his professional activity to investigating what Freud had called "the black tide of mud of occultism." Although the scientific establishment scorned the notion that occult phenomena were worthy subjects for investigation, the romantics had managed to generate excitement about hypnosis, mesmerism, somnambulism, precognition, and spiritualism, so that a man with Jung's family history, personal experiences, predisposition, and natural gifts was not alone in his proc-livities. After he separated from Freud, Jung immersed himself in Gnostic and Neoplatonic texts and in Eastern philosophy. Befriended by the cele-brated German Orientalist Richard Wilhelm, he explored Chinese alchemy and the *I Ching*, the ancient Chinese method of divination. Jung took this oracle quite seriously as a revelation of unconscious knowledge. In prepar-ing the introduction to Wilhelm's book, *The Secret of the Golden Flower*, Jung found the link he had been searching for, between ancient Gnosticism and modern thought, in European alchemy. He identified himself with another Swiss doctor-metaphysician, Paracelsus, who had enriched the sixteenth century with his esoteric lore. "Magick is a Great Hidden Wisdom—Reason is a Great Open Folly," he had taught.

Paracelsus' observation that Eastern and Western alchemy were really concerned with psychic states rather than with chemical states confirmed Jung's perspective of the unconscious as a reservoir of collective as well as personal images. This collective unconscious explained the presence of archetypes—myths and symbols that were made up of "universal dynamic forms." Though there were similar archetypes in all races and throughout all the ages, there were also perceived differences between races, because of their different evolutions. The Jew, for instance, because he was rootless, needed to "reduce everything to its material beginnings." That was why the simple reduction by Freud and Alfred Adler of all psychic phenomena to primitive drives was gratifying to the Jew, though "thoroughly unsatisfying to the Germanic mentality," which still (in 1918) had "a genuine barbarian in [it] who [was] not to be trifled with." Said Jung: "The fact is, our unconscious is not to be got at with over-ingenious and grotesque interpretations. The psychotherapist with a Jewish background awakens in the Germanic psyche not those wistful and whimsi-cal residues from the time of David, but the barbarian of yesterday, a being for whom matters suddenly become *serious* in the most unpleasant way. . . ."

By the time the Nazis came to power, this sort of distinction caused Jung some embarrassment—not, to be sure, with the champions of National Socialism. The new study of psychoanalysis had to go through a process of *gleichgeschaltung*, i.e., conformity to the Party line. Jung's mysticism was far more congenial to the philosophy of Aryanism than Freud's "Jewish science." Jung understood and shared the romantic sensibility which craved for pagan purification. In 1923 he had written:

> . . . we cannot possibly get beyond our present level of culture unless we receive a powerful impetus from our primitive roots. But we shall receive it only if we go back behind our cultural level, thus giving the suppressed primitive man in ourselves a chance to develop. How this is to be done is a problem I have been trying to solve for years. . . . the existing [edifice] is rotten. We need some new foundations. We must dig down to the primitive in us, for only out of the conflict between civilized man and the Germanic barbarian will there come what we need: a new experience of God. . . .

Jung came under the influence of the German Indologist Jakob Wilhelm Hauer, an authority on Kundalini yoga and number-symbolism. Hauer was head of the Nordic Faith movement, which barred Freemasons, Jews, and colored people from membership. He lectured at Eranos, a Swiss esoteric school for Jungians, on the racial unconscious and its symbolism. When the Nazis came to power, he gave an impassioned talk on the SS hero and Hitler, the "genius of our people." Jung, in his essay, "Wotan," later mentioned that Hauer's group "aims at the religious renaissance of the nation out of the hereditary foundations of the German race" and advised the "German Christians" to join Hauer's "decent and well-meaning people . . . intelligent enough not only to *believe* but to *know* that the god of the *Germans* is Wotan and not the Christian God."

When the president of the international German Medical Society for Psychotherapy, located in Germany, resigned because of the Nazi takeover in 1933, Jung filled the post by remote control from Switzerland and assumed the editorship of its official publication, the *Zentralblatt für Psychotherapie*. Its December 1933 issue was graced with a commitment by the new Reichsführer of psychoanalysts, Professor M. H. Göring, the nephew of Hermann Göring, to "Adolf Hitler's fundamental book, *Mein*

Kampf" and "to contribute to the work of the people's chancellor to educate the German people for the spirit of heroism and sacrifice." And Göring gratefully acknowledged: "Thanks to the fact that Dr. C. G. Jung accepted the presidency on June 21st, 1933, it has been possible to continue the scientific activity of the Association and of its periodical."

For that same issue, Jung wrote an introduction which he later had many opportunities to defend:

> The differences which actually do exist between Germanic and Jewish psychology and which have long been known to every intelligent person are no longer to be glossed over, and this can only be beneficial to science. In psychology more than in any other science there is a "personal equation," disregard of which falsifies the practical and theoretical findings.

Though he went on to state that he was no more depreciating "Semitic psychology" than he would if he talked of the Chinese in terms of Oriental psychology, his editorial in no way hurt him with the Nazis. The General Medical Society, although international in membership, was dominated by the Germans. Its publication was put out in Germany, and the managing editor and staff were German. Jung had given orders that the issue which caused him such embarrassment be "for exclusive circulation in Germany," but the managing editor had disobeyed him. Jung said: "The incident is naturally so incriminating as to put my editorship seriously in question."

But he defended his position in the March 28, 1934, letter to Max Guggenheim:

> If you disregard the persecutions of the Jews in Germany, you must admit that there is a medical Society there which is very important for us in Switzerland. It is therefore not a matter of indifference what happens to psychotherapy in that country. . . . As a psychotherapist I cannot be indifferent to the future of psychotherapy. Its development in Germany will also be crucial for us. Freud once told me, very rightly: "The fate of psychotherapy will be decided in Germany." To begin with it was doomed to absolute perdition because it was considered wholly Jewish. I have broken this prejudice by my intervention and have made life possible not only for the so-called Aryan psychotherapists but for the Jewish ones as well. What with the hue and cry against me it has been

completely forgotten that by far the greatest number of psychotherapists in Germany are Jews. People do not know, nor is it said in public, that I have intervened personally with the regime on behalf of certain Jewish psychotherapists. If the Jews start railing at me this is shortsightedness in the extreme and I hope you will do what you can to combat this idiotic attitude. The existence of the Society for Psychotherapy, which has very many Jewish members, is now assured, also the membership of Jewish doctors. Actually the Jews should be thankful to me for that. . . .

Although he had already made it clear in 1918 that he believed in psychological differences between Jews and Aryans, 1933 was an inopportune moment to reiterate such a thesis. Anyone of Jewish descent had been purged from the German civil service that spring. Other professions were closing to Jews, and with 6 million unemployed, there was a scramble for their jobs. While Jung was not a Nazi, he understood the Nazis' paganism. He also understood their antipathy to Freud, whom he felt to be lacking in spiritual concerns. The Nazi psychiatrist Kurt Gauger reiterated this point of view:

Freud is the scientist, only the scientist: Jung is the ethician. One could also call him a seer, in the deepest and most reverent sense of the word. Jung is the poet among psychologists. His subconscious is full of living forms with whom one speaks and consorts like human beings, who can give counsel and warn, with whom one tries to be on a good footing because otherwise they may become "angry." Jung's psychology is a demonology. . . . Primordial wisdom has it that one can disarm a demon, even make a servant of him, if one knows his name. . . .

Freudian psychology incorporates all the advantages and dangers of the Jewish spirit, Jungian psychology all those of the Germanic soul.

Freud is atheistic; Jung, not in terms of doctrine but in terms of attitude, is marked by a Catholic piety. . . .

Jung protested that he was not anti-Semitic, that he had courageously chosen to talk about that which was on everyone's mind, that Jews could not be insulted since he had made no value judgments, and that it was the failure to make distinctions which leveled everything and caused hatred between people. He was not for tarring everyone with the same brush. He fought Freud's psychology, he said,

because of his materialistic and intellectualistic and—last but not least—
irreligious attitude and not because he is a Jew. Insofar as his theory is
based in certain respects on Jewish premises, it is not valid for non-Jews.
Nor do I deny my Protestant prejudice. Had Freud been more tolerant of
the ideas of others I would still be standing by his side today. I consider
his intolerance—and it is this that repels me—a personal idiosyn-
crasy. . . . Infinite nuances are needed if justice is to be done to human
beings.

To "accept the conclusions of a Jewish psychology," then, "as generally valid," was a "quite unpardonable mistake."

Jung's branding of Freud's psychoanalysis—a technique evolved out of
this "Jewish psychology"—as a "Satanic" doctrine capable of "murder-
ing souls" did not injure his growing reputation. Many famous artists and
writers had flocked to him for soul salvation. In 1939, the Mellons were
converted. Andrew Mellon's interest in the occult resulted in a huge
collection of books on the subject, stretching back to antiquity, which he
donated to Yale. The Mellons set up the Bollingen Foundation to publish
Jung's work.

After the atrocities of the Holocaust became public knowledge, Jung's
outrage against the Nazis was genuine. Still, his assistant, H. G. Baynes,
gave the Jews some unpleasant moments by theorizing, in *Germany
Possessed*, without reasonable evidence that Hitler's natural father had
been a wealthy Viennese Jew:

By far the greater portion of the wealth and power of Austria was, at that
time, in the hands of the Jews, and they were also guilty of an unfeeling
ostentation of wealth and luxury while half Vienna was starving. One
can understand, therefore, how the mind of the boy [Hitler] saw the Jews
as the worldly possessors who lay coiled about the wealth of his
motherland.

Hitler's "uncanny shrewdness," "political flair," and "taste in lavish
interior decoration," "handsome furniture," and "rare things," as well as
his "amazing political opportunism" were the result of his Jewish blood.
Hitler, in a word, was "the Wandering Jew," "the man accursed"
because he had spurned "the jewel of great price," Christ's teaching.

Not until 1945 did Jung publicly comment again upon events in Germany, and then to present himself as a prophet who had foreseen the

"collective psychic murder." Now it was the "German psychology" which he dissected. The German, charged Jung, instead of purging himself by admitting his guilt, shifted his responsibility for the crime and refused even to acknowledge that he had ever been a Nazi. He "dolled up" his inferiority feeling with "pseudo-scientific race-theory," which "did not make the extermination of the Jews any more acceptable."

About his own collusion Jung said nothing.

Criticism for his aid to the cause of what he believed would be a "Germanic, Jew-free psychotherapy" has now died down, and in the present atmosphere of receptivity to occultism, his ideas, books, and disciples are in the vanguard, enjoying great prestige.

It is difficult, however, to accept his defense that he was simply trying to save a young science. The December 1933 *Zentralblatt* issue occasioned a number of alarmed letters from colleagues. His answer to Max Guggenheim, on March 28, 1934 (see above), was representative.

What is more likely, the reigning attitudes in Germany expressed mystical affinities with which Jung was very much at home. There were several areas of compatibility between Jung and the Nazis: alchemy, astrology, the Grail legend, the symbolism of the runes, medieval mysticism, anti-bolshevism, and so forth. His high degree of tolerance for the "shadow" side of human nature, a necessary complement to reason, may have caused him to cast the Nazis in a romantic light. Like them, he was not afraid to explore the hidden recesses of the unconscious for ancient secrets so great and fearful, as he said, "that the world is grateful to Freud for having proved 'scientifically' (what a bastard of a science!) that one has seen nothing behind [the door]. . . ."

The Nazis were the new barbarians who would purge civilization of its clotted, stultifying elements. They were the antidote to the civilized man, who had advanced too rapidly, "which is why we have become lopsidedly intellectualistic and rationalistic and have quite forgotten that there are other factors which cannot be influenced by a one-track rational intellect."

If Jung was able, at least for a while, to add his prestige to the Nazis' *weltanschauung*, it was because of their common occult ground. His thinking rendered him susceptible to their apocalyptic visions of Hitler as a magical shaman with a spiritual mission. To the extent that he enhanced their credibility, if only in their own minds, he strengthened faith in the "hero cult."

CHAPTER 14

Jehovah as Satan

Jehovah . . . was a creature of darkness, hence an Evil
God. . . .

—Louis Israel Newman, *Jewish Influence
on Christian Reform Movements*

The Jews have figured as scapegoats many times in history. They have
been hounded and massacred. This has been laid to their obstinacy in
clinging to their religion and image as God's chosen people; to their
rejection of Christ; to their economic superiority; and to their presumed
unique psychology. But there is one peculiar motive for the extermination
policy of the Nazis which has hitherto escaped attention. It suggests itself
when we view the Nazis in the light of occult thinking: The mystical
teachings of Guido von List, Lanz von Liebenfels, and Rudolf von Sebottendorff were modern restatements of Gnosticism.

When the apocalyptic promise of Christ's resurrection was broken, the
Gnostics sought to return men to God by another route, more Oriental than
Hellenist. They devised a dualistic cosmology to set against the teachings
of the early Christian Church, which, they claimed, were only common
deceptions, unsuited for the wise. The truth was esoteric. Only the properly
initiated could appreciate it. It belonged to a secret tradition which had
come down through certain mystery schools. The truth was, God could
never become man. There were two separate realms—one spiritual, the

other material. The spiritual realm, created by God, was all good; the material realm, created by the demiurge, all evil. Man needed to be saved, not from Original Sin, but from enslavement to matter. For this, he had to learn the mystical arts. Thus Gnosticism became a source for the occult tradition.

A famous medieval Gnostic sect, the Cathars, came to identify the Old Testament god, Jehovah, with the demiurge, the creator of the material world and therefore the equivalent of Satan. Within Gnosticism, then, existed the idea that the Jewish god was really the devil, responsible for all the evil in the world. He was opposed to the New Testament God. The Cathars tried to eliminate the Old Testament from Church theology and condemned Judaism as a work of Satan's, whose aim was to tempt men away from the spirit. Jehovah, they said, was the god of an earth "waste and void," with darkness "upon the face of the deep." Was he not cruel and capricious? They quoted Scripture to prove it. After promising that the Tower of Babel would be built, he dispersed the builders. He rained down a deluge; ravaged Sodom and Gomorrah; circumcised his male people; encouraged animal sacrifice; insisted on strict observance of a day of rest; made two sexes, to battle each other; issued an edict to Adam which was transgressed out of ignorance or imperfection, then cursed his sinful creation.

The New Testament God, on the other hand, was light. He declared that "there is neither male nor female," for everyone was united in Christ. He blessed his creation, which was good and perfect and without sin.

These two gods, obviously, had nothing in common.

The synagogue was regarded as profane by Christians. The Cathars—themselves considered heretical by the Church—castigated Catholics for refusing to purge themselves of Jewish sources; Church members often blamed the Christian heresy on Jewish mysticism, which was considered an inspiration for Gnostic sorcery.

But Gnostic cosmology, though officially branded "false," pervaded the thinking of the Church. The Jews were widely thought to be magicians. It was believed that they could cause rain, and when there was a drought, they were encouraged to do so. Despite the displeasure of the Roman Popes, Christians, when they were in straitened circumstances, practiced Jewish customs, even frequenting synagogues.

To the medieval mind, sorcery had an everyday reality, and the sorcerer was living proof of Satan's power. The Jew, with his strange customs, was suspected of practicing black magic in his most innocent rituals.

Tossing a bit of earth behind oneself or rinsing the hands after a funeral; binding the head and overturning the bed during mourning; attaching a *mezuzah* (a scroll, inscribed with Biblical passages, placed in a small case, as a reminder of faith in God) to the doorpost—all these were mystifying to the Christian, and filled him with dread. Jews grew so sensitive about the accusations of sorcery that they were often exempted by their rabbis from some of their customs out of fear of arousing suspicion, "for this is a matter of life and death, since they accuse us and persecute us." A Jewish group, bringing gifts to Richard I's coronation in London in 1189, touched off a conflict which lasted more than six months. It was thought that they used witchcraft on the new monarch.

Their reputation for supernatural powers—enhanced by their Biblical reputation for interpreting dreams—gave them a psychological edge over Christians in their practice of the healing arts. Moreover, ancient Arabic and Greek medicine was available to the Jews through their versatility in languages and their travels; and immunity from Church dogma made them look elsewhere than to miraculous relics and cures. Paradoxically, the scientific medical skill which the Jews amassed further confirmed their image as sorcerers. Thus the Christian who acknowledged the Jewish physician's superiority by seeking him out for a cure risked the consequences of a mortal sin. In this and a multitude of other ways, the Jew embodied all of the medieval ambivalence toward Satan.

Never before had Satan played the starring role that he did in that era. Under the shadow of Gothic spires, Satan skulked, waiting to pounce on unsuspecting souls. He tormented them with pestilence and portents, but also with visions of incredible beauty, because the old devil was infinitely adaptable and could appear in the guise of one's fondest dream. Terror-stricken by a Church which preached sin and sorrow, trapped in a world which wallowed in both, the Christian did not love God so much as he feared the devil. As the Italian scholar Arturo Graf puts it in *The Story of the Devil*:

Satan is the child of sadness . . . in order that he may grow and thrive, there is need of shadows, of the mysteries of sin and of sorrow, which like a funeral shroud enfold the religion of Golgotha. Satan is the child of fear; and terror dominates the Middle Ages. Seized with an unconquerable dread, the souls of men . . . fear the physical world, opposed to the world of the spirit, and its irreconcilable foe; they fear life, the perpetual incentive and tinder-box of sin; they fear death, behind which yawn the uncertainties of eternity. Dreams and visions torment men's minds. The ecstatic hermit, kneeling long hours in prayer before the doorway of his cell, sees flying through the air awe-inspiring armies and riotous hordes of apocalyptic monsters; his nights are lighted up by flaming portents; the stars are distorted and bathed in blood, sad omens of impending evil. In seasons of pestilence that mow men down like ripened stalks of grain, are seen darts, hurled by invisible hands, cleaving the air and disappearing with hissing sound; and ever and anon, across the face of terror-stricken Christendom runs, like a tremor presaging the world's end, the sinister word that Antichrist is already born and is about to open the fearful drama foretold in the Apocalypse.

If God seemed absent, Satan was present everywhere, not only in curses but in prayers, and the Church, intimately acquainted, gave him full publicity. What was the Church without the devil and hell? As Graf points out: "The Church made good use of Satan, employed him as a most effective political tool, and gave him all possible credit; since what men would not do through love of God or in a spirit of obedience, they would do through fear of the Devil." Men may have hated Satan, but they also recognized him as the real ruler of the physical world. He had all the power. One couldn't help admiring him for that and wish for some of it oneself.

Though the medieval Christian persecuted the Gnostics, it is scarcely surprising that he accepted their view of the Jew as the child of Satan. Despite outward appearances, it seemed that the Jew was not really a human creature. He did not *smell* human. It was said that he ate Christian children; that horns even grew out of his head. In certain periods in Vienna, he was required to wear a horned hat; in France, a horn-shaped figure on his badge. Satan, in his portraits, has decidedly Semitic features. The Jew seemed to the Christian, as well as to the Gnostic, to enjoy the kingdom of this world, whatever he might expect in the next. His failure to accept Christ was, therefore, to be expected. What better proof of his partnership with Satan than his practical involvement with worldly goods? A Gnostic axiom declared: "The world's money is the corruption of the soul." Since the material world was the devil's domain, it was necessarily perverted. All matter was vile. Christians and Gnostics believed that the Jew was attracted by matter and adept at controlling it: hence, his inordinate love of ostentatious luxury and his financial genius.

The body, too, belonged to Satan. It was the prison of the soul. Physical man was a brute—one of Satan's nicknames was God's Ape—and it was through the passions, particularly sex, that man's greatest demonic temptations came. Here, also, the Jew was considered the exemplary demonic being, living only for his appetites, not the least the sexual appetite. The simplest way for the devil to invade souls was through possession, and the most intimate form of possession was through sexual intercourse. It was not uncommon for the devil to unite himself with human beings this way, and all the evil in the world was proof of the number of diabolical children thus begotten. Furthermore, in the Gnostic view, procreation itself was always evil. Since matter was Satan's creation, the struggle against evil could only triumph, ultimately, with the cessation of new life. This was too much to ask of weak mortals, but it was a direction toward which to tend.

Gnosticism, going by name of Hermetism in the Renaissance and Reformation, practiced magic and meditation to try to free the spirit from the body. The Age of Enlightenment was not particularly hospitable to the occult tradition, but Gnosticism found new advocates among nineteenth-century Germans. The original "fall into matter," the creation of Jehovah, which had unloosed all the evil in the world, was now given a "scientific" explanation, in light of Darwin's theories; popularizers gave the layman to understand that the inequality of races was due to a tragic flaw carried in the blood. Madame Blavatsky held, in *The Secret Doctrine*, that the Gnostics "were right in regarding the Jewish God as belonging to a class of lower, material and not very holy denizens of the invisible world.

". . . For the creation of those wretched races, in a spiritual and moral sense, which grace our globe, no high divinity could be made responsible, but only angels of a *low hierarchy*, to which class they relegated the Jewish God, Jehovah." [italics hers.]

The Jewish God, furthermore, was identical with Cain, Son of Eve by Satan, said Madame Blavatsky.

The anti-Semites embraced this with glee, and the concept of Aryanism was wedded to the forces of light. Nature, they said, decreed that the union of Aryan and Semite resulted in a hybrid monstrosity, psychically sterile. Since "bad blood drives out good," an Aryan woman mating with a Jew was sure to bear only Jewish children. Proponents of hypnotism and suggestion accounted for "Jewish" traits by the observation that a mother's thoughts were mentally transmitted to the fetus. "Nature is and remains essentially aristocratic and punishes implacably all attempts upon the purity of the blood," said Ludwig Buchner. The Jews were originally a crossbreed, argued Houston Stewart Chamberlain, and "their existence is sin, their existence is a crime against the holy laws of life; this, at any rate, is felt by the Jew himself in the moments when destiny knocks heavily at his door. Not the individual but the whole people had to be washed clean, and not of a conscious but an unconscious crime." Anti-Semitism, then, was the instinctive "wisdom" of the Aryan race, which, as the "fittest," sought to survive. To explain the Jew's survival, his "inability to disappear," one commentator fell back on his material wealth, which he hid "under the appearance of misery."

Geographers, sociologists, political scientists, and Orientalists made common cause in attributing the differences between the German and the Jew to the contrast between desert and forest. The racial soul, developed over eons, led to the softness, parasitism, sterility, and alienation from nature which was manifest in the Jew, and the strength, courage, creativity, and love of nature displayed by the German. "Biological philosophers" such as Theodor Fritsch, Jörg Lanz von Liebenfels, and Guido von List preached "racial hygiene" to inflamed Aryans worrying about the contamination of their blood. Within a few decades, men of learning and propagandists succeeded in implanting in the Germans a "scientific racism" which gave them a warrant for genocide.

The greatest obstacle in the way of extermination, religious sentiment, was swept aside by divorcing Jesus from his origin as a Jew and making him the ancestor of the Germanic tribes, a sort of Siegfried-Christ. German racists took the Gnostic view that Christianity must separate itself from the Old Testament, and they printed "a mass of 'revelations' of every kind (such as the 'unveiling of the secrets' of Holy Writ or of Runic lore or of Paradise itself)," as Leon Poliakov points out in *The Aryan Myth*.

Of course, a great deal of this religious questing was associated with speculations and experiments in occult phenomena or in theosophy and spiritualism. . . . But it was only in Germany that they took such an aggressively pagan as well as patriotic and nationalistic turn. The inevitable spongers who climbed on to the band-wagon earned a living by . . . forging documents to prove the Aryanism of Jesus.

The Jew, "the devil incarnate of human decadence," as Richard Wagner called him, had made a "Judaeo-barbaric jumble of the world," and only a blood purification rite would keep civilization going.

Wagner transposed esoteric themes into music and turned on generations of Germans to the real meaning of the struggle between the Jew and the

Aryan. One of his operatic themes was the quest for the Holy Grail, a mystery in the ancient Gnostic tradition that had been revealed in the songs of the Cathar troubadours and was understandable only to those who had ears to hear.

Hitler was one. He worshipped Wagner, and expounding on the opera *Parsifal*, confided to Hermann Rauschning:

> Behind the absurd externals of the story, with its Christian embroidery and its Good Friday mystification, something altogether different is revealed as the true content. . . . pure, noble blood, in the protection and glorification of whose purity the brotherhood of the initiated have come together. The king is suffering from the incurable ailment of corrupted blood. The uninitiated but pure man is tempted to abandon himself in Klingsor's magic garden to the lusts and excesses of corrupt civilization, instead of joining the *elite* of knights who guard the secret of life, pure blood.

Only the "truly pure and noble" would partake of the "eternal life granted by the grail," Gnostic symbol for hidden knowledge of immortality.

Rauschning observed that to Hitler the Jew represented "the very principle of evil," and that in his "esoteric doctrine" the "mythical prototype of humanity," the Jew, must be "the irreconcilable enemy of the new, the German, Chosen People. One god excludes the other." There was an "actual war of the gods." Rauschning, ignorant of esoteric doctrine, assumed that Hitler meant this symbolically, but Hitler assured him:

> No! It's the sheer simple undiluted truth. Two worlds face one another— the men of God and the men of Satan! The Jew is the anti-man, the creature of another god. He must have come from another root of the human race. I stood the Aryan and the Jew over against each other, and if I call one of them a human being I must call the other something else. The two are as widely separated as man and beast. Not that I would call the Jew a beast. He is much further from the beasts than we Aryans. He is a creature outside nature and alien to nature.

We can understand more fully the Nazis' intense identification with the Middle Ages in the light of their Gnostic attachment. A reporter in Munich in 1936 observed colored pictures of Hitler in the silver garb of the knights of the Holy Grail. The pictures were withdrawn by the Nazis after a short while. SS training classes presented material on the Grail, on knighthood, on alchemy, and on Gnostic history. Nazi antipathy to the Church confused Christians, who failed to recognize in the reference to a paganized Christ the ancient Gnostic heresy. As Hitler told Goebbels in Rauschning's presence:

The peasant will be told what the Church has destroyed for him: the whole of the secret knowledge of nature, of the divine, the shapeless, the daemonic. . . . We shall wash off the Christian veneer and bring out a religion peculiar to our race. And this is where we must begin. Not in the great cities. . . . There we shall only lose ourselves in the stupid godless propaganda of the Marxists: free sex in nature and that sort of bad taste. The urban masses are empty. Where all is extinguished, nothing can be aroused. But our peasantry still lives in heathen beliefs and values. . . .

Most important, the central doctrine of nazism, that the Jew was evil and had to be exterminated, had its origin in the Gnostic position that there were two worlds, one good and one evil, one dark and one light, one materialistic and one spiritual.

This sheds light on an otherwise incomprehensible recurring theme within Nazi literature, as, for example, "The Earth-Centered Jew Lacks a Soul," by one of the chief architects of Nazi dogma, Alfred Rosenberg, who held that whereas other people believe in a Hereafter and in immortality, the Jew affirms the world and will not allow it to perish. The Gnostic secret is that the spirit is trapped in matter, and to free it, the world must be rejected. Thus, in his total lack of world-denial, the Jew is snuffing out the inner light, and preventing the millennium:

Where the idea of the immortal dwells, the longing for the journey or the withdrawal from temporality must always emerge again; hence, a denial of the world will always reappear. And this is the meaning of the non-Jewish peoples: they are the custodians of world-negation, of the idea of the Hereafter, even if they maintain it in the poorest way. Hence, one or another of them can quietly go under, but what really matters lives on in their descendants. If, however, the Jewish people were to perish, no nation would be left which would hold world-affirmation in high esteem—the end of all time would be here.
. . . the Jew, the only consistent and consequently the only viable yea-sayer to the world, must be found wherever other men bear in

themselves . . . a compulsion to overcome the world. . . . On the other hand, if the Jew were continually to stifle us, we would never be able to fulfill our mission, which is the salvation of the world, but would, to be frank, succumb to insanity, for pure world-affirmation, the unrestrained will for a vain existence, leads to no other goal. It would literally lead to a void, to the destruction not only of the illusory earthly world but also of the truly existent, the spiritual. Considered in himself the Jew represents nothing else but this blind will for destruction, the insanity of mankind. It is known that Jewish people are especially prone to mental disease. "Dominated by delusions," said Schopenhauer about the Jew. . . . To strip the world of its soul, that and nothing else is what Judaism wants. This, however, would be tantamount to the world's destruction.

This remarkable statement, seemingly the rantings of a lunatic, expresses the Gnostic theme that the spirit of man, essentially divine, is imprisoned in an evil world. The way out of this world is through rejection of it. But the Jew alone stands in the way. Behind all the talk about "the earth-centered Jew" who "lacks a soul"; about the demonic Jew who will despoil the Aryan maiden; about the cabalistic work of the devil in Jewish finance; about the sinister revolutionary Jewish plot to take over the world and cause the decline of civilization, there is the shadow of ancient Gnosticism. The medieval concept of the Jew as sorcerer was apparent in Hess's announcement, after his capture by the British, that the Jews were in possession of a secret power to hypnotize people and make them act against their will.

And like the medieval inquisitors, the Nazis felt no qualms of conscience about burning the Satanic Jews. Only, they substituted crematoria for fagots and stakes.

CHAPTER 15

Making an Obedient Mass

The Germans are vigorously submissive. They employ
philosophical reasonings to explain what is the least
philosophic thing in the world, respect for force and the fear
which transforms that respect into admiration.

—Madame de Staël

It is too easy to say that the German soul was predisposed to totalitarian-
ism. Even if the people were inured to submissiveness through iron
discipline for generations, they were never, before Hitler, genocidal
maniacs.

Since World War II, several books have appeared which, while not
dealing directly with the Nazis, are of invaluable aid in explaining how
ordinary people can be transformed into automata, devoid of conscience or
reason. They help us to understand, not only the Nazis, but millions of
disciples of movements in Western countries today who, almost overnight,
are weaned from their customary behavior and attachments and indoctrinated with irrational beliefs. They are *The True Believer* by Eric Hoffer,
The Mind Possessed by William Sargant, and *The Rape of the Mind* by
Joost Meerloo.

What is the formula for producing pliant followers?

Take people, not wholly preoccupied with subsistence, who despair of
being happy either in the present or in the future. They feel the sharp cutting

edge of frustration. Either through some personal defect or because external conditions do not permit growth, they are eager to renounce themselves, since the self is insupportable.

Many German men were in this position at the end of World War I. They came home to a civilian life without purpose, in which they had no part. In the chaos and collapse, vast armies of uprooted people felt threatened by the war's economic and social aftermath. National Socialism gave them a chance for a fresh start. As Eric Hoffer points out:

> People who see their lives as irremediably spoiled cannot find a worth-while purpose in self-advancement. The prospect of an individual career cannot stir them to a mighty effort, nor can it evoke in them faith and a singleminded dedication. They look on self-interest as on something tainted and evil; something unclean and unlucky. Anything undertaken under the auspices of the self seems to them foredoomed. Nothing that has its roots and reasons in the self can be good and noble. Their innermost craving is for a new life—a rebirth—or, failing this, a chance to acquire new elements of pride, confidence, hope, a sense of purpose and worth by an identification with a holy cause. An active mass movement offers them opportunities for both. If they join the movement as full converts they are reborn to a new life in its close-knit collective body, or if attracted as sympathizers they find elements of pride, confidence and purpose by identifying themselves with the efforts, achievements and prospects of the movement.
>
> To the frustrated a mass movement offers substitutes either for the whole self or for the elements which make life bearable and which they cannot evoke out of their individual resources.

The movement, in turn, encourages self-renunciation. It does not attract the individual who believes in himself, nor does it care to; on the contrary, he is precisely the individual whom it ridicules. It popularizes the idea that the private person who finds his own satisfactions is halting the progress of civilization. But to the person with the unwanted self, unable to believe in himself, the movement provides something larger to believe in. As Hitler pointed out: "Monkeys put to death any members of their community who show a desire to live apart. And what the apes do, men do too, in their own manner."

The movement also provides justification. To those who find no meaning or purpose in life, it says: "The world is out of joint, not you" or

"The world that most people inhabit is an illusion." No longer alone in its misery, the frustrated mind now has company, which includes even those who protest that they are happy, because it is taught to see through that so-called happiness.

As one Nazi, Karl-Heinz Schwenke, a tailor, described it:

I had ten suits of my own when I married. Twenty-five years later, when their "democracies" got through with me in 1918, I had none, not one. I had my sweater and my pants. Even my Army uniform was worn out. My medals were sold. I was nothing. Then, suddenly, I was needed. National Socialism had a place for me. I was nothing—and then I was needed.

The movement also provides a suitable outlet for the pent-up rage which frustrated people feel, against themselves and the world. It fans that rage and honors it. The believer's rage may actually increase in proportion to what he has had to give up to become part of the movement: his former life, his friends, his family, his privacy, his judgment, sometimes even his name and worldly goods. He is willing, even eager, to make these sacrifices and more, of course, because by making them he can slough off the undesirable self. He receives, in return, an artificial sense of worth. His stature grows through involvement with the group. He is assured that he is great, one of the chosen.

SS men were held together by the idea that they were a sworn brotherhood of the elect. Their mystic rituals gave them special obligations, some too abhorrent to contemplate, but also special privileges.

The believer becomes a fanatic. As a frustrated person, incapable of acting in his own best interests, he never had a firm grip on reality. He can enter into the fantasy life of the movement and act on behalf of impossible dreams, which impose less risk on his fragile ego than he would encounter if he were to tussle with personal hurdles. He gets a sense of omnipotence, too, from tackling world-shaking tasks.

Running away from an acceptance of his own nature and the world as it is, the believer is prone to credulity. He believes *because* it is impossible. He can be persuaded by the irrational and led by the nose by charlatans. It is easy for him to become irresponsible, since he is not following his own will.

Rudolf Hoess, commandant of Auschwitz, was the perfect exemplar of will-lessness. As he confessed at Nuremberg: "I had nothing to say. I could only say *Jawohl*! We could only execute orders without thinking about it. . . . from our entire training the thought of refusing an order just didn't enter one's head, regardless of what kind of order it was."

Since life has been irremediably spoiled for the believer, he has relatively little hesitation about spoiling it for others. This gives him an advantage. He can be unscrupulous under the disguise of idealism. His self-righteousness permits him to convince himself that he is destroying people for their own good. Josef Goebbels felt it his duty "to unleash volcanic passions, outbreaks of rage, to set masses of people on the march, to organize hatred and despair with ice-cold calculation." Eric Hoffer explains such inhumanity:

> It seems that when we are oppressed by the knowledge of our worthlessness we do not see ourselves as lower than some and higher than others, but as lower than the lowest of mankind. We hate then the whole world, and we would pour our wrath upon the whole of creation.
>
> There is a deep reassurance for the frustrated in witnessing the downfall of the fortunate and the disgrace of the righteous. They see in a general downfall an approach to the brotherhood of all. Chaos, like the grave, is a haven of equality. Their burning conviction that there must be a new life and a new order is fueled by the realization that the old will have to be razed to the ground before the new can be built. Their clamor for a millennium is shot through with a hatred for all that exists, and a craving for the end of the world.

This recalls Alfred Rosenberg's argument that "the denial of the world needs a still longer time in order to grow so that it will acquire a lasting predominance over affirmation of the world," and his equation of the Jew with world affirmation.

To be bored is also to be potentially an easy mark for a movement. It provides the meaning and purpose which are gone from the life of the isolated individual, burdened with freedom. As one young Nazi put it just before World War II, "We Germans are so happy. We are free of freedom."

What sort of social milieu is it that breeds people who want to be free of freedom?

Precisely that which has increasingly prevailed since the nineteenth century: a mass society in which the individual is atomized and counts for very little. He stands completely alone. His ties with the community, the family, the kinship group have been broken. Paradoxically, he needs them more than ever, because individual life becomes increasingly absurd and incoherent the more mass society advances.

Uprooted from village and ancestral loyalties and shifted to the anonymous city, the individual suffers culture shock: The old values are out of place in the hostile, competitive world. As an isolated person, no longer part of a settled group whose norms he accepted, he is uncertain and empty—unless he is an independent thinker or a creative spirit, in which case he may feel himself well rid of the influence of the group. But with the encroachment of mass society, it is less and less likely that he will be able to think or create. A philologist, specializing in Middle High German, described the situation candidly to Milton Mayer (*They* Thought *They Were Free*:

> . . . suddenly, I was plunged into all the new activity, as the university was drawn into the new situation; meetings, conferences, interviews, ceremonies, and, above all, papers to be filled out, reports, bibliographies, lists, questionnaires. And on top of that were the demands in the community, the things in which one had to, was "expected to" participate that had not been there or had not been important before. . . . it consumed all one's energies. . . . You can see how easy it was, then, not to think about fundamental things. One had no time. . . . The dictatorship, and the whole process of its coming into being, was above all diverting. It provided an excuse not to think for people who did not want to think anyway. . . . Most of us did not want to think about fundamental things and never had. There was no need to. Nazism gave us some dreadful, fundamental things to think about—we were decent people—and kept us so busy with continuous changes and "crises" and so fascinated, yes, fascinated, by the machinations of the "national enemies," without and within, that we had no time to think about these dreadful things that were growing, little by little, all around us. Unconsciously, I suppose, we were grateful. Who wants to think?

Through mass education and mass communication, the individual is propagandized and molded into conditioned responses, like one of Pavlov's dogs. His innate ability to figure things out for himself atrophies, with predictable consequences.

To soften the pain of emptiness, he is drowned in entertainments, which offer him hero-surrogates who are able to live for him. Eternally occupied either as hustler, machine, or spectator, he seldom has a moment to notice that he cannot think, feel or live; that his life is petty, shabby, and totally without meaning; that his authorities are deceitful and manipulative, his society disintegrating, his relationships hollow, and worst of all, that nothing is being done to remedy these horrors.

The irony is that the individual in mass society *has* only himself. The authority of his parents has been undermined. He has moved from the soil where he was born and experienced certain local allegiances. His work is inhuman and mechanical. No meaning, responsibility, or dignity attaches to it. It requires his participation, but actually develops passivity. It regiments him, and he remains an apathetic machine. He is dependent on his job, and in periods of economic insecurity, glad to have it, but he feels diminished by it.

His relationships lack intimacy and affection. He can no longer trust anyone. He must have answers that will explain the problems of his life. Yet, because he has been trained *not* to think for himself, he faces a void, and his life becomes unendurable.

Human beings can't stand being unimportant. Most will readily accept the idea of further and further "massification"—the greater leveling and equality which is evidence of greater democracy—as a sign of progress. Mass society is symbolized by modernism and egalitarianism, two popular myths of progress. In Germany, this egalitarianism culminated in Hitler's boast that

> sixty thousand men have outwardly become almost a unit, that actually these men are uniform not only in ideas, but that even the facial expression is almost the same. Look at these laughing eyes, this fanatical enthusiasm, and you will discover how a hundred thousand men in a movement become a single type.

What does the movement offer the faithful?

Nothing less than a new life. His rebirth is sometimes symbolized in a new name, exotic and foreign, to make the change of identity tangible. Now there is certainty. He knows exactly what is expected of him. Within a circumscribed set of rules, all is permitted: rage without guilt, relief from responsibility, the assertion of superiority over others.

He knows what action is required of him in the present and can look forward to a millennial future as well. There is no more ambiguity. The conflicts, tensions, self-criticisms, and doubts that assail the rest of us are washed away, and he enjoys a state of equilibrium. He is no longer a

passive participant. Righteously, he looks down at those whom he formerly felt to be superior. The same society which scorned him now is forced to
recognize that his beliefs are important. The mass man becomes a power in
the world. Rudolf Hess, the melancholy student who became deputy leader
of the Third Reich, remained grateful to the end. As he testified at
Nuremberg:

> It was granted to me for many years of my life to live and work under
> the greatest son whom my nation has produced in the thousand years of
> its history. Even if I could I would not expunge this period from my
> existence. I regret nothing. If I were standing once more at the beginning
> I should act once again as I did then, even if I knew that at the end I
> should be burnt at the stake. No matter what men do, I shall one day
> stand before the judgment seat of the Almighty. I shall answer to him,
> and I know that he will acquit me.

In exchange for this miraculous transformation, the individual willingly
subjects himself to a thorough brainwashing, through which his old beliefs
and personality are eradicated. He may never be aware that he is being
brainwashed. It may happen instantly or gradually, but he puts absolute
trust in the leaders of the movement. The group becomes the good father he
may never have had, the proxy whom he depends on to solve all his
problems, the authority to which he owes obedience. From the moment he
is captured, he identifies with the group and begins to think as they do.
Their common undertaking insures that he will never have to shoulder any
personal blame for failure or shortcomings. So long as he behaves according to the rules, he will be accepted. The rules are clear and consistent,
or seem to be.

The Germans were used to compulsion from early childhood. Rudolf
Hoess's reminiscence is fairly typical, and makes his subsequent acqui-
escence in running Auschwitz more plausible:

> It was constantly impressed upon me in forceful terms that I must obey
> promptly the wishes and commands of my parents, teachers, priests,
> etc., and indeed of all grown-up people, including servants, and that
> nothing must distract me from this duty. Whatever they said was always
> right.
>   These basic principles on which I was brought up became part of my
> flesh and blood. I can still clearly remember how my father, who on

account of his fervent Catholicism, was a determined opponent of the
Reich Government and its policy, never ceased to remind his friends
that, however strong one's opposition might be, the laws and decrees of
the State had to be obeyed unconditionally.

From my earliest youth I was brought up with a strong awareness of
duty. In my parents' house it was insisted that every task be exactly and
conscientiously carried out. Each member of the family had his own
special duties to perform.

The group is beyond criticism. Its realm is sacred. Even if a man has
convictions which run counter to those of the movement, he can still be led
to act in a manner which contradicts his own beliefs, either because his will
is weak or because he is the victim of certain techniques which cause his
will to be transcended. He can say, with Hermann Göring, "I have no
conscience! Adolf Hitler is my conscience!" or "It is not I who live, but
the Führer who lives in me."

It is important to examine these techniques if we are to understand how
people can be made to follow a Führer wherever he may lead.

The proselyte is isolated at first. No free exchange with unbelievers is
allowed. He is cut off from ties of loyalty with the past. His family and
friends are discredited. Feelings of exclusivity are encouraged.

His mind is barraged with repetitive propaganda until it is made weary.
The indoctrination may go on uninterruptedly for sixteen hours or more a
day, for weeks on end. Even if the proselyte rejects what he hears, argues
against it, or falls into apathy, the Pavlovian conditioning ultimately
seduces him, and he surrenders to the training.

Mechanical drill, rhythmical marches, dance rituals, and repetitive
chanting are also effective in breaking down resistance.

The English psychiatrist William Sargant could better grasp how Hitler
was able to bring even intelligent Germans into "a condition of intellectual
and emotional subjection" through "mass rallies, marching and martial
music, chanting and slogans and highly emotional oratory and ceremony"
after witnessing the subservience of certain African tribes to their leaders
and seeing their powerful initiation rites:

Whether in a "primitive" tribe or at school or in the army, the process
is essentially the same. Severe stress is imposed on the new recruit, by
subjecting him to arbitrary and frightening authority, by bewildering
him, abusing or ill-treating him, by telling him that his old values and

sentiments are childish, and so inducing in him a state of unease and suggestibility in which new values can easily be drummed into him, and he recovers his self-confidence by accepting them. The initial conditioning techniques may have to be reinforced from time to time by further conditioning procedures, and follow-up indoctrination is considered most important in all types of religious or other conversion.

Once the proselyte has been broken down and sensitized, his thinking and feelings can be manipulated, and delusions implanted. He falls under the suggestive power of the group and accepts its distortions as objective truth.

Most people are suggestible and can be hypnotized against their will, obeying commands even when they go against the grain. Dr. Sargant observes:

It is not the mentally ill but ordinary normal people who are most susceptible to "brainwashing," "conversion," "possession," "the crisis" . . . and who . . . fall readily under the spell of the demagogue or the revivalist, the witch-doctor or the pop group, the priest or the psychiatrist, or even in less extreme ways the propagandist or the advertiser.

In the suggestible state, the proselyte may attribute divine powers to his leader and accept dogmas which he might have rejected in a more normal state. Some of the men closest to Hitler, for example, acknowledged that they believed in his divinity. Himmler's masseur, Felix Kersten, relates that he once answered the phone and heard Hitler's voice before passing the phone on to Himmler, who exclaimed: "You have been listening to the voice of the Führer, you're a very lucky man." Himmler told Kersten that Hitler's commands came "from a world transcending this one" and "possessed a divine power." It was the "Karma" of the German people that they should be "saved" by "a figure of the greatest brilliance" which had "become incarnate" in Hitler's person.

And even disbelievers and scoffers can also come to accept irrational dogmas—through contagion, imitation or sudden conversion.

Beliefs have the power to infect. The onlookers at a mass rally, where emotions are being stirred up, often feel the same intensity of excitement that the participants feel. We can "catch" ideas that are completely foreign to us. In early Judaism, for example, there was no concept of a demonic force. God was responsible for both good and evil. But with influences from Iran, Egypt, and Greece came a tendency to explain evil as the work of demons. Soon after, people began to see manifestations of evil spirits everywhere, and "every misfortune, every illness, and particularly, under the name of *possession*, all disorders of the nervous system were ascribed to them," according to Charles Guignebert in *The Jewish World in the Time of Jesus*.

Hitler's early speeches were so mesmerizing that even people who were repelled by his ideas felt themselves being swept along. The playwright Eugène Ionesco mentions in his autobiography that he received the inspiration for *Rhinoceros* when he felt himself pulled into the Nazi orbit at a mass rally and had to struggle to keep from developing "rhinoceritis."

We "catch" ideas, too, because we want to be like others, particularly when we want *not* to be our despised selves. If we're satisfied, we don't need to conform, but if we're not, we imitate people whom we admire for having greater judgment, taste, or good fortune than we do. Obedience itself is a kind of imitation. Through conformity, the person who feels inferior is in no danger of being exposed. He's indistinguishable from the others. No one can single him out and examine his unique being. Conformity, in turn, sets him up to be further canceled out as an individual, to have no life apart from his collective purpose. This gives a movement tremendous power over the individual. Even intelligent people are not immune from the desire to conform. Heinrich Hildebrandt, a schoolteacher who was anxious to hide his liberal past, joined the Nazi party, and to his own disgust, found himself "proud to be wearing the insignia. It showed I 'belonged,' and the pleasure of 'belonging,' so soon after feeling excluded, isolated, is very great. . . . I belonged to the 'new nobility.' "

Hoffer observes:

Above all, he [the true believer] must never feel alone. Though stranded on a desert island, he must still feel that he is under the eyes of the group. To be cast out from the group should be equivalent to being cut off from life.

This is undoubtedly a primitive state of being, and its most perfect examples are found among primitive tribes. Mass movements strive to approximate this primitive perfection, and we are not imagining things when the anti-individualist bias of contemporary mass movements strikes us as a throwback to the primitive.

Sudden conversions, which may happen through hypnosis, emotional shock, despair, or exhaustion, can bring people into movements. William Sargant believes an apparently well-balanced person, "dominated by hypnoid and slightly suggestible brain activity," may suddenly give up his "previous intellectual training and habits of rational thought," to accept "ideas which he would normally find repellent or even patently nonsensical." Sargant is convinced that a heightened state of suggestibility accounts for many cases of demonic possession, or for sudden salvation. The history of mysticism offers instances of extreme opinions instantly reversed. The critical faculty is suspended, and what was formerly believed to be black is now white, and vice-versa.

Once the believer has been taken over by one of these means, it is difficult for him to revert to his former self. In a sense, collective totalitarian thinking can be compared with schizophrenia. In both, there is, says Joost Meerloo in *The Rape of the Mind*, a "loss of an independent, verifiable reality, with a consequent relapse into a more primitive state of awareness." In both, thought and action are arrested at an infantile level of development.

Since the totalitarian denies man's dynamic nature, views him simply as a submissive robot, and provides this robot with one single, simple answer to all the ambivalences, doubts, conflicts, and warring drives within him, all attempts to dislodge the official clichés clash with those same clichés. The believer's isolation in a fortress of other delusional thinkers gives him no opportunity for clear thought or contact with other influences. He is immune to reasonable propositions. He is convinced that he *is* reasonable, and that his enemies are not. Having burned his bridges behind him, broken with his family and old friends, he cannot go back. He is committed to his involvement in the group. To renounce it would be to repudiate himself. It would also mean giving up all the psychic benefits of omnipotence. His personality and prejudices have become crystallized around a set of actions and dogmas. They are irreversible. Any external stimulus which threatens to penetrate his armor and make him see the absurdity or injustice of his position is rationalized to further harden his rigidity. He has joined the movement at least partly because it handed him stereotypes in place of his vague notions and saved him from having to think things out for himself. Any stimulus which evokes a symbol causes a reflex action. With his weakened conscience and consciousness, he can no longer respond spontaneously, however he may appear to be doing so. He has *become* the movement. All thoughts and feelings that are at odds with it are snuffed out. This is what gives the believer the air of a one-dimensional man. He lacks depth. There is a limited range of possibilities open to him. If one wants, therefore, to convert him back to an autonomous human being, one finds that there is nobody at home. His mind is shut tight against new ideas. The slogans and ready-made judgments he has absorbed stretch forward into infinity. The believer is protected for all time. Within his sacred circle, all other knowledge is taboo. One might say that the most telltale sign of a believer is his refusal to examine ideas other than the divine commandments which have been implanted in him. One can't get to him because he will not and cannot engage in dialogue. What is particularly maddening about him is that, sterile and unimaginative, he masquerades as an exemplary man, an objective guide eager to spread enlightenment.

The ability to exercise his own judgment, having atrophied, is never restored. Even if he should drop out of one group, he will quickly seek and find another. Like a drug addict who needs his fix, he cannot live without his clichés.

At Nuremberg after the war, Allied examiners were shocked to see how unrepentant some of the Nazis were. Julius Streicher cried "Heil Hitler! Heil Hitler! Heil Hitler!" at his execution, until the opening of the trap door muffled his voice. Arthur Seyss-Inquart declared, to the last, that Hitler remained "the man who made Greater Germany a reality in history." Rudolf Hoess, by his own admission "completely filled, indeed obsessed" with his monstrous goal, was not guilty of arrogance when he proudly declared that "Auschwitz became the greatest human extermination center of all time." He was one of the countless ordinary men who had been turned into a believer. He gave validity to Hitler's contention "that by the clever and continuous use of propaganda a people can even be made to mistake heaven for hell, and vice versa, the most miserable life for Paradise." As Hitler knew better than perhaps anyone else: "The essence of propaganda consists in winning people over to an idea so sincerely, so vitally, that in the end they succumb to it utterly and can never again escape from it."

We need not, however, look as far back as Nazi Germany for examples of people undergoing personality changes and extreme shifts in ideology. We can learn from present-day American groups.

CHAPTER 16

The Dangers of Occult Thinking

If we believe absurdities, we shall commit atrocities.

—Sarvepalli Radha Krishnan

Men who are ignorant of history may be condemned to repeat its lessons, as the American philosopher George Santayana observed. But the reverse is true too. We often need the experience of the present to shed light on the events of the past, so that we are better able to guide our lives in the future.

If we are to ask now, more than a generation later, how normal people could have committed the Nazi atrocities, we need only look at the normal people in American cults today. This may seem a harsh comparison; the parallels are certainly not universally applicable. Still, it would not be unfair to say that the same sort of normal people who obeyed the crazy commands of the Nazi hierarchy are today obeying the crazy commands of some contemporary cult leaders. To be sure, those commands, apart from certain Satanic cults, do not call for ritual murder. Not yet, at any rate. But none of us should feel too comfortable with so many of our compatriots so willing to suspend independent judgment, and so ill equipped to exercise that judgment.

Membership in occult groups in America today has reached epidemic

161

proportions. Some people take this as an omen that Satan is hard at work; others, that God is. The groups take many different forms: Satanism, witchcraft, pseudoscience, mind-control, mysticism, Christian, pagan. Most are not as innocent as they seem, as we are beginning to find out.

The one which has most often been compared with the Nazis is, of course, the Charles Manson cult, with its murderous violence and sadomasochistic sex. All the Satanic groups express a great admiration for Hitler. Anton LaVey, the leader of the Church of Satan, probably has the largest collection of Nazi memorabilia in America. LaVey dedicated his book, *The Satanic Bible*, to a number of people, including the Nazi geopolitician "Karl Haushofer, a teacher without a classroom."

In the case of other groups, there are less obvious parallels. The Reverend Sun Myung Moon came from Korea to save tens of thousands of American youth, who hail him as the Messiah. In gratitude, they have left their families to give their energies totally to his Unification Church. Growing numbers of abandoned parents are banding together, forming organizations to try to use legal means to get their children deprogrammed, protesting to the government that "destructive cults and their strategy of alienation" have "psychologically kidnapped" their offspring. The parents chose Moon's cult to begin their offensive with. Once having found grounds for prosecution, they will move on to other groups.

Despite parental pressures, there are few dropouts among the "Moonies." Moon's brainwashing techniques work amazingly well, particularly in light of the fact that he appeals to Americans in the Korean language, that he looks and behaves like a provincial businessman, that he indulges in Byzantine luxury while preaching asceticism, and that his sales pitch is markedly uninspired. His commercial enterprises, encompassing a Korean industrial conglomerate which brings in $15 million a year, real estate holdings in New York worth more than $11 million, and various operations serviced by Moonies without pay, are all tax-exempt.

The young disciples, some graduates of prestigious colleges, give their free labor gladly, doing whatever they are told by their superiors in the hierarchy, in return for which they receive a responsibility-free life. They hawk the glad tidings of the new Messiah on city street corners and college campuses. Their clothes, lodgings, and thoughts are provided by the Church. A sample of Moon's wisdom, from his writings:

"I am your brain."

"What I wish must be your wish."

"My mission is to make new hearts, new persons."

"Satan is everywhere and you are vulnerable to his attack."

". . . Satan confronted Jesus, working through the Jewish people. . . ."

"During the second World War, 6 million people were slaughtered to cleanse all the sins of the Jewish people from the time of Jesus."

"Of all the saints sent by God, I think I am the most successful one."

"The time will come . . . when my words will almost serve as law. If I ask a certain thing it will be done."

"The whole world is in my hand, and I will conquer and subjugate the world."

"By putting things in order, we can accomplish God's will. All obstacles to this world must be annihilated."

"Our strategy is to be unified into one with ourselves, and with that as the bullet we can smash the world."

Many people drift into Moon's groups after drug experiences. The emotional "high" in meetings and meditation is likened to the drug high. The evangelist group on the corner is always on the lookout for the lonely figure in the crowd. After a brief discussion, they invite the prospect to join them at an introductory lecture, enclose him in a circle of friendship. Next comes a weekend workshop, with relentless hours of indoctrination in a syncretism of Eastern mysticism, occultism, and instant psychology. The recruit is given nonstop tender, loving care. Hints are dropped about Moon's supernatural powers. Those who go on to a week-long workshop will probably stay, donate their lives to the Church, and be stamped with identical robot-like smiles. An observer, watching a prayer session, compared it to a voodoo ceremony.

Moon was a relatively late arrival on the wave that brought in planeloads of gurus from India, Japan, China, and Tibet. In their own countries they were as familiar as a bowl of rice, whereas in America they were exotic, but for all that, they caught on here as fast as franchised fast-food chains and were advertised in a similar manner, as part of the growing "growth" movement, which has become a profitable industry.

The McDonald's of that movement, as one writer called it, is TM, whose Maharishi Mahesh Yogi, with white wraps and irrepressible giggles, looks like a bearded infant, but has turned out to be cunning enough to harness "big science" by converting quantum physicists, astronauts, psychologists, and medical researchers. He has also been clever enough not to alienate parents, but has converted them as well. TM, he declares, is not a religion. Yet the initiation ceremony is Hindu, and each individual is assigned a mantra which, he is told, has special properties suitable to him alone. He is never to repeat this mantra to anyone. The initiator who assigns the mantra has only a few vital statistics to guide his choice. Those who take up TM themselves do not know—or will not say—how the appropriate mantras are distributed. "Maybe," one psychiatrist-convert told me, "it's done on the basis of astrological signs." One TM scientist, Dr. Harold Bloomfield, flatly declares that using the wrong mantra might kill you.

Scientology, another variation with science-fiction neologisms, has a native-born chief, L. Ron Hubbard, former science-fiction writer. His group conditions its people to believe that if you so much as *oppose Scientology* it might kill you. One does not drop out of such a group lightly. Some former Scientologists have met with mysterious deaths, and some enemies of Scientology—"suppressives" or "potential trouble sources," they are called—have been harassed. There are all sorts of unsavory rumors. Yet Father Hubbard's cupboard is far from bare. Some years ago, a reporter figured his "take" to be $140,000 a week. It has undoubtedly grown since then.

L. Ron Hubbard's most formidable competitor at the moment is an even sharper salesman who once earned his living training people to sell encyclopedias door-to-door. He was born Jack Rosenberg, but changed his name to Werner Hans Erhard. A former student of Scientology and Mind Dynamics, he eventually packaged his own "growth" elixir, called est (for Erhard Seminars Training), which uses Storm Trooper tactics to bring people to enlightenment. Est people insist that it's incorrect to think of the process as brainwashing, since no coercion is used. But if one considers brainwashing to include the breaking down of old beliefs and the systematic indoctrination in new beliefs, then est, like so many other contemporary cults, is brainwashing, and doing it successfully. The trainee has only a vague idea of what to expect when he comes for the first and second weekend seminars, because people who have been through the training are told not to spoil it for newcomers by telling them in advance what happens.

What does happen is awesome or frightening, depending on your frame of reference. Two hundred and fifty people sit in uncomfortable chairs for

sixteen hours a day over two weekends, with only two breaks a day—
determined by the trainer—for eating, going to the bathroom, smoking,
talking, moving about, or note-taking. Harangued and insulted, the participants are brought to the edge of despair. Group dynamics are so
skillfully manipulated as to convert them, in the end, to estian bliss. The
results are impressive. People move out of static grooves, are more open
and lighthearted. Why, then, feel at all uneasy? Because, as one trainee put
it:

> I have seen people take est and become like robots, give up their
> freedom, and deny their healthy instincts. These people, fortunately, are
> relatively few in number—and can, I suppose, be written off as the
> "fringe" of followers that seem to crop up with every new group today.
> But they are the extreme result of what est is all about: est "trains" us to
> cope and adapt and follow the rules of society; it teaches us how to live
> and function under totalitarianism. What makes est successful is not its
> basic message—which is, after all, nothing new—but the positive re-
> sponse of thousands of us to the authoritarian way in which that message
> is packaged, sold, and practiced day to day.

This is in no way an exhaustive survey of the existing occult groups in
America today. There are thousands upon thousands of others, some better
known and more powerful than the ones mentioned, others hidden and
secret, with a few hundred or a few thousand followers, closed to the
general public. As one writer, John C. Cooper, observed in *Religion in the
Age of Aquarius*, it's "a seller's market for anyone who comes with a
vision—no matter how myopic—of how the universe hangs together
around the groping individual." Millions of people belong to what are
called "the new religions" and more are joining daily. These are not fads.
On the contrary, they represent the beginning of a mass "consciousness"
movement which is helping many people to solve personal and social
problems. It is certainly helping the leaders of these groups to cash in on
those problems. Not all are powerful personalities or charismatic figures.
Some are downright repulsive. The Guru Maharaj Ji, Perfect Master of the
Divine Light Mission, is a fat, blank-faced teen-ager with a penchant for
costly possessions. His own mother renounced him and tried to promote his
elder brother as savior, instead. Two of his disciples seriously wounded a
newspaperman who threw a pie in the Maharaj Ji's face because he'd
always wanted to throw a pie in the face of God. Adverse publicity does not

seem to have affected the devotion of disciples, who still kiss his feet.
Gross or slick, ascetic or fleshpot, every leader's claims to special favor
from the gods are validated by his disciples. Moon, Hubbard, and the
Maharishi Mahesh Yogi offer photographs of themselves which disciples
relate to in the same way that Catholics relate to photographs of paintings of
Jesus Christ. The transition from teacher to Messiah can sometimes easily
be charted. Hubbard's passage from one to the other is still not quite
complete, but he is definitely in transit, according to George Malko, "off
on a new tangent, rhetorically asking his followers 'Who is the Messiah?'
only to answer with a parable involving a powerful, barrel-chested man
with red hair," remarkably like himself.

Both Hubbard and Erhard are Machiavellian enough to be careful to
wipe out potential competition when they see it in their more ambitious
followers. The Messiah business has many advantages. You don't need
academic training or degrees. No financial investment is necessary, and the
financial rewards are unreal. No mortal work is more prestigious. Even an
unexalted past is no deterrent. Moon, Hubbard, and Erhard have managed
to rationalize theirs, just as nineteenth-century prophets did.

Though each group has its own distinctive style, people often move
freely from one to another. Some observers have been surprised at the
attraction of former radical revolutionary Rennie Davis to the Divine Light
Mission. Jerry Rubin, the former Yippie leader, has sampled such a
smorgasbord of cults that he's been labeled a "guru whore." If the true
believer seeks to lose or validate himself in a movement, a spiritual
movement can serve as well as a political one.

The spiritual and political often merge with one another. Esoteric leaders
have been known to act as advisers to governments. Reverend Moon, who
has enjoyed the protection of the South Korean government, prepares his
disciples to be ready to lay down their lives for that government, the
"fatherland" of the Unification Church. He came to America with more
influence and hard cash than is usual at the beginning of religious careers.
He organized a political arm in Washington, D.C., called the Freedom
Leadership Foundation, which sponsored talks and publications dedicated
to fighting communism in America and supporting the South Korean
government. Church publications reproduce photographs of Moon taken
with Senators Hubert Humphrey, James Buckley, Edward Kennedy, and
Strom Thurmond. When Nixon met his Watergate, Moonies prayed for the
government and held demonstrations in Washington. Moon, claiming to be
under orders from God, took full-page ads in major newspapers throughout

the country: "This nation is God's nation. The office of the President of the United States is therefore sacred. . . . God has chosen Richard Nixon to be President of the United States." With Moon's move to America, he seems to have given up the idea that the Koreans are the chosen people of the twentieth century and now bestows that honor on the Americans.

The Maharishi Mahesh Yogi courts the military as well as the National Aeronautics and Space Administration. A few army generals and astronauts have become enthusiastic disciples. Major General Franklin M. Davis is excited over the prospect of getting the whole U.S. Army to meditate. It would help solve the drug problem, he believes.

To young people, the new religions are compatible with radical politics—usually of the right—because they view both as anti-Establishment. John C. Cooper observes:

> Perhaps the connecting link of politics and magic in our times is the unconscious awareness of many young people that while the external actions of a hippie spellcasting and the rhetoric and hoopla of a political convention are only window dressing, somewhere within the group, and perhaps in a way not responsive to the wishes of either the majority or the minority of those involved, decisions that will affect the course of human events are being made. When men feel that for all their hard work and all their good wishes they are cheated out of a share of control over the destiny of their group, then superstition grows in the area of man's spirit and rebellion arises in the area of man's actions.

It is significant that the modern occult groups grew out of the drug scene—replaced it, in effect. Drugs were not just a way out of insupportable reality, but a religious experience, search, and preoccupation. It is noteworthy that contemporary gurus boast of providing the only successful means for getting young people off drugs. Either drugs or the meditation the gurus offer is a means of finding a way to feel at home in technological society without conflicting with its operation.

The drug scene, like the modern cults, had its own jargon, rituals, and communal sharing. With both, an inner core of deeply committed practitioners drew to itself a fringe of imitative onlookers who copied the life-styles and formulas. The drug adventure has really been preempted by the spiritual search for meaning, creating the same ecstasies, visions, confusion of the senses, and synthetic paradise. Instead of passing around a joint, some young people are now chanting together. But they still live in a "holy" place completely alien to the uninitiated, who are repelled by their orgiastic delirium, and whom they accuse of not understanding because they "haven't been there."

It is significant, too, that the modern occult movement began simultaneously with America's involvement in the distasteful war in Vietnam, which intensified the feeling of impotence. The occult movement will help to prepare its followers for the "brave new world" that's coming. Many observers have already remarked on the similarity in manner of people within each individual group, and among groups in general, even those which purport to make people free. They have been compared with robots, automata, and zombies, for good reason. Despite the promise that their training will increase their capacity for alertness and their ability to face reality, the influence exerted by the group, whether intended or not, is the opposite. One cannot be successfully propagandized without losing some essential part of individual humanity. It is odd to talk with some of the cult members about a speculative point—say, for instance, the astral plane— and see how very wise and absolute they appear in discussing an irrational tenet which they have never examined. And when one asks "Why?" in a class in esoteric philosophy, one is told, " 'Why?' is the devil's question."

No doubt, some cults really do help some people. They are frightening nonetheless. Occultists themselves are frightened. The hypnotic effect is powerful, whatever the quality of the particular leader or doctrine.

When we remember that the Nazi party arose out of the merger of mystical groups, there is cause for even more distress. These groups considered themselves sacred. Faith in a holy cause had taken possession of them. They were completely incapable of objectivity. What they did was not seen by many of them as evil. This pathological blindness convinced them that they were participating in the superhuman task of ridding the world of a menace.

There were those ambitious men, too, who saw an opportunity to advance in the hierarchy. Once they climbed to a certain height, they had a large stake in the Nazi movement. In maintaining the supremacy of the group, they had individual power. Obedience and devotion insured their success. Like the ancient Aryan conquerors of India, they created a society so structured that no citizen could do anything without official sanction. The Chandala, the lowest Aryan caste, became, figuratively, the Jew.

The Brahmins, using the authority of the Vedas, created, through the laws of Manu, a totalitarian organization which corrupted the wisdom of

Eastern philosophy and so invaded every area of private Hindu life that it was impossible to go to the bathroom without obeying certain strictures. They squeezed the heart out of India. Twentieth-century Aryans, emulating the Brahmins, set up their own ideas of caste, but instead of favoring hereditary aristocracy, made it possible for the credulous, ambitious, and unscrupulous to rise to the top.

We have an opportunity, in watching contemporary groups evolve before our eyes, to recreate what must have happened in Germany before and after World War I, to fill in gaps in our understanding, and to recognize the German people as similar to ourselves. They were swept along by "prophets" like Lanz, List, and Sebottendorff. The well-to-do among them gave them financial backing, which must have reassured Lanz, List, and Sebottendorff in their beliefs in themselves as Messiahs and heralds.

Then, as now, people put their trust in a single man, revered him as a saint, loved him like a father. They were prepared to follow him into the bowels of Hell. Hitler was said to have had a magnetic personality, but this is hardly necessary, nor was he seen in this light by some of those who were immune to his message. There are leaders preaching to multitudes today who have no discernible power to attract, other than the will of people to believe in them. And no matter how ridiculous the edicts handed down from on high—perhaps *because* they are ridiculous—believers are eager to justify and rationalize.

I have been present at meetings where proselytes, presumably sane and rational, accepted without question irrational doctrines presented portentously, believing that they were receiving revealed truth.

I have also been present at a protest rally sponsored by parents who had lost their children to the Pied Piper of the Unification Church. It was a pitifully thin crowd compared with the twenty-five thousand who would appear at Yankee Stadium that same evening for Reverend Moon's rally. The parents and deprogrammed ex-Moonies spoke to the press. They repeated again and again: "You won't believe this. How could you? It's all so strange, so irrational. It sounds like science fiction. But don't kid yourself. It's really happening. You must alert people to the danger."

I didn't know if their stories had much credibility to others, but to me, after all I had learned about the Nazis, they had the ring of authenticity.

One parent told me that her daughter, a wholesome, bright, dynamic college student, had been sucked into the group by attending one of its weekends. She was idealistic. She wanted to help combat the drug problem. After one week of indoctrination, she was hooked on Moon. "I didn't recognize her when I saw her again," said her mother. "She was like a robot. She'd been thoroughly brainwashed. She'd taken on a whole set of new ideas. It was the most frightening thing you can imagine."

The brainwashing process was systematic. Trainees were taught to practice "heavenly deception" in canvassing for funds for Moon. "Heavenly deception" encompassed the use of subliminal suggestion on prospective contributors. Moonies were indoctrinated to smile in a particular way. Their parents' lives, they were told, depended on their movement. They were to save the world through their mission, and eventually they would be groomed to enter politics and take over world government.

"All we talked about was taking over," an ex-Moonie told me. "This was an army we were in. We screamed that we were heavenly bullets. We were going to take over the government and then the country without one bullet. We would take over and rule the world."

Gradually, they were made to see that their families were Satanic. Mail from home was kept from them. They were shifted about the world and kept from contact with friends and relatives. If they tried to drop out other Moonies were dispatched to bring them back. The Unification "family" was not a happy community, however it might have appeared to outsiders. Fatigued and ill-fed, they were constantly competing to meet fund-raising quotas. The rigorous program, which entailed unexpected reveilles in the middle of the night and flashlit mountain marches, sometimes led to physical accidents, which were hushed up. Moonies did not really get along with each other. Hysteria, anxiety, guilt, and terror resulted from the pressure.

The parents at the protest rally, determined to get their children back, paraded placards which read:

REMEMBER HITLER

NO MORE HITLERS . . . STOP MOON

MOON IS DESTROYING AMERICA'S YOUTH

"Aren't they taking themselves too seriously?" one reporter asked. "Moon's group seems so innocuous."

"The Hitler Youth began by raising money, selling flowers and candy most aggressively. Parents in Germany must have felt this way about their kids," I answered. "And with good reason."

Sources Quoted

This list contains only sources not included in the bibliography.

Alleau, René, *Hitler et les sociétés secrètes*, Editions Bernard Grasset (Paris, 1969).

Blavatsky, H. P., *The Secret Doctrine*, Vol. II, Theosophical University Press (Pasadena, Calif., 1974).

Cooper, John C., *Religion in the Age of Aquarius*, The Westminster Press (Philadelphia, Pa., 1971).

Dicks, Henry V., *Licensed Mass Murder*, Basic Books, Inc. (New York, 1972).

Ebon, Martin, *Prophecy in Our Time*, New American Library (New York, 1968).

Fest, Joachim C., *The Face of the Third Reich*, Pantheon Books (New York, 1970).

————, *Hitler*, Harcourt Brace Jovanovich, Inc. (New York, 1974).

Fraenkel, Heinrich, "Is Hitler Youth Curable?", *New Republic*, September 18, 1944.

Graf, Arturo, *The Story of the Devil*, Macmillan Co. (New York, 1931).

Grunberger, Richard, *Hitler's SS*, Delacorte Press (New York, 1970).

Hartshorne, E. Y., *German Youth and the Nazi Dream of Victory*, Farrar & Rinehart, Inc. (New York, 1941).

Hitler, Adolf, *Hitler's Secret Conversations 1941-1944*, Farrar, Straus & Young (New York, 1953).

————, *Mein Kampf*, Houghton Mifflin Co. (Boston, Mass., 1943).

Hohne, Heinz, *The Order of the Death's Head*, Coward-McCann, (New York, 1970).

Jaffe, Aniela, *From the Life and Work of C. G. Jung*, Harper & Row (New York, 1971).

Leasor, James, *The Uninvited Envoy*, McGraw-Hill Book Co., Inc. (New York, 1962).

List, Guido von, *Die Religion der Ario-Germanen in ihrer Esoterik und Exoterik*, Guido von List-Verlag (Vienna, 1910).

Lowenthal, Marvin, *The Jews of Germany*, Longmans, Green & Co. (New York, 1936).

Mayer, Milton, *They Thought They Were Free*, University of Chicago Press (Chicago, Ill., 1955).

Merkl, Peter H., *Political Violence Under the Swastika*, Princeton University Press (Princeton, N.J., 1975).

Pauwels, Louis, and Bergier, Jacques, *The Dawn of Magic*, Anthony Gibbs & Phillips (London, 1960).

Rauschning, Hermann, *Men of Chaos*, G. P. Putnam's Sons (New York, 1942).

————, *The Voice of Destruction*, G. P. Putnam's Sons (New York, 1940).

Ravenscroft, Trevor, *The Spear of Destiny*, G. P. Putnam's Sons (New York, 1973).

172   Sources Quoted

Schellenberg, Walter, *Hitler's Secret Service*, Pyramid Publications, Inc. (New York, 1974).
———, *Memoirs*, A. Deutsch (London, 1956).
Sebottendorff, Rudolf von, *Bevor Hitler Kam*, Deufula-Verlag Grassinger & Co. (Munich, 1933).
Shirer, William L., *The Rise and Fall of the Third Reich*. Simon & Schuster (New York, 1960).
Speer, Albert, *Inside the Third Reich*, Macmillan Co. (New York, 1970).
Stern, Paul J., *C. G. Jung: The Haunted Prophet*, George Braziller, Inc. (New York, 1976).
Walsh, Edmund A., *Total Power*, Doubleday & Co., Inc. (New York, 1948).
Webb, James, *The Occult Underground*, Open Court Publishing Co. (La Salle, Ill., 1974).
Wykes, Alan, *Himmler*, Ballantine Books, Inc. (New York, 1972).

Selected Bibliography

Hanfstaengl, Ernst, *Hitler: The Missing Years*, Eyre & Spottiswoode (London, 1957).
Heckethorn, Charles W., *Secret Societies of All Countries*, Vol. II, New Amsterdam Book Co. (New York, 1897).
Hoffer, Eric, *The True Believer*, Harper & Row (New York, 1951).
Howe, Ellic, *Astrology: A Recent History Including the Untold Story of Its Role in World War II*, Walker & Co. (New York, 1968).
Jung, C. G., *Civilization in Transition*, Pantheon Books (New York, 1964).
———, *Letters 1906-1950*, Princeton University Press (Princeton, N.J., 1973).
———, *Psychology and Religion: West and East*, Pantheon Books (New York, 1958).
Kersten, Felix, *The Memoirs of Dr. Felix Kersten*, Doubleday & Co., (New York, 1947).
Kubizek, August, *The Young Hitler I Knew*, Houghton Mifflin Co. (Cambridge, Mass., 1955).
Langer, Walter, *The Mind of Adolf Hitler*, Basic Books, Inc. (New York, 1972).
Laqueur, Walter Z., *Young Germany*, Basic Books, Inc. (New York, 1962).
Ludecke, Kurt Georg, *I Knew Hitler*, Charles Scribner's Sons (New York, 1937).
Meerloo, Joost A. M., *The Rape of the Mind*, World Publishing Co. (Cleveland, Ohio, 1956).
Mosse, George L., *The Culture of Western Europe* (Chicago, 1961).
———, ed., *Nazi Culture*, Grosset & Dunlap (New York, 1966).
Mumford, Lewis, "The Revolt of the Demons," *The New Yorker*, May 23, 1964.
Phelps, Reginald H., " 'Before Hitler Came': Thule Society and Germanen Orden," *The Journal of Modern History*, Vol. XXXV, No. 3. (September 1963).
———, "Hitler and the *Deutsche Arbeiterpartei*," *American Historical Review*, Vol. LXVIII, No. 4 (July 1963).
Podmore, Frank, *From Mesmer to Christian Science*, University Books, Inc. (Secaucus, N.J., 1963).
Poliakov, Leon, *The Aryan Myth*, Basic Books, Inc. (New York, 1974).
Reiss, Curt, *Total Espionage*, G. P. Putnam's Sons (New York, 1941).
Roberts, Stephen H., *The House That Hitler Built*, Harper & Bros. (New York, 1938).
Sargant, William, *The Mind Possessed*, J. B. Lippincott Co. (New York, 1974).
Smith, Bradley F., *Henrich Himmler: A Nazi in the Making, 1900-1926*, Hoover Institution Press (Stanford, California, 1971).
Trachtenberg, Joshua, *The Devil and the Jews*, Meridian Books (New York, 1970).

Waite, Robert G. L., "Adolf Hitler's Anti-Semitism: A Study in History and Psychoanalysis," in Benjamin B. Wolman, ed., *The Psychoanalytic Interpretation of History*, Basic Books, Inc. (New York, 1971).

Walther, Gerda, "Hitler's Black Magicians," *Tomorrow*, Vol. IV, No. 2.

Webb, James, *The Occult Establishment*, Open Court Publishing Co. (La Salle, Ill., 1976).

Webster, Nesta H., *Secret Societies and Subversive Movements*, Boswell Printing & Publishing Co., Inc. (London, 1924).

Wulff, Wilhelm, *Zodiac and Swastika*, Coward, McCann & Geoghegan (New York, 1973).

Index

Ku Klux Klan, 18
Kurz, Heinz, 45

Labor Service (youth group), 110-11
Lagarde, Paul de, 105, 108
Langbehn, Julius, 105, 108
Langer, Walter, 119-20
Lanz von Liebenfels, Jörg, 5, 7, 14, 17-21, 24,
28, 47-48, 55, 95, 105, 118, 140, 145, 169
Büch der Psalmen Teutsch, Das, 48
changes name, 19
early life, 19-20
influence on Hitler, 21, 24, 48
New Templars' Breviary, The Psalms in
German, 20
Theozoologie, 20. See also Germanen Orden;
Order of the New Templars; Ostara
Laquer, Walter Z., Young Germany, 106
La Vey, Anton, 2, 63
Satanic Bible, The, 162
Lawrence, D. H., 130
Lebensborn (maternity homes), 113-15
Lebensraum theory, 62-63
Lehmann, Julius, 41
Leviné-Nissen, Eugen, 44
Levien, Max, 44
Ley, Robert, 97-98, 103
Ley, Willy, Rockets, Missiles, and Men in
Space, 79-80
List, Guido von, 5, 7, 13-14, 17, 22-25, 28,
47-48, 55, 95, 105-6, 107, 140, 145, 169
Religion der Ario-Germanen, Die, 118. See
also Armanen Brotherhood; Germanen
Orden
Littleton, C. Scott, 99
Ludecke, Kurt, 52, 54, 67
Ludendorff, Erich, General, 3, 4
Ludendorff, Mathilde, 106
Lueger, Karl, 22, 51

Magdeburg Project, 79-80
Maharaj Ji, 165-66
Maharishi Mahesh Yogi, 163, 166, 167
Manson, Charles, 2, 162
mass movements, dynamics of, 150-58, 165, 166
Mayer, Milton, They Thought They Were Free,
153
Meerloo, Joost, Rape of the Mind, The, 149, 159
Mellon, Andrew, 138
Mesmer, Franz Anton, 117
Messiah and Messianism, 3, 5, 13, 47, 52, 60,
162, 166, 169
Middle Ages, as Nazi influence, 7, 9, 14-15, 20,
28, 85, 88, 99-100, 105, 142, 146-47
Milgram, Stanley, obedience experiments, 46-47

Moltke, Helmuth von, 41
Moon, Sun Myung, 162-63, 166-67, 169-70
"Moonies," 162, 166-67, 169-70
Mosse, George L., Culture of Western Europe,
The, 105
Müller, Gustav, 106
Mumford, Lewis, 130
Münchener Beobachter, Der, 38, 57
Munich:
Beer Hall Putsch, 53, 61, 67
Communist activity in, 6, 37, 39, 43-44
secret cults in, 6, 40-42
Vier Jahreszeiten hotel, 37-38, 39
Mussolini, Benito, 60, 103

Napoleon, 8
National Liberal party, 40
National Socialist German Workers' Party
(NSDAP), 42-43. See also Nazi party
National Socialist Monthly, 71
Natural Man, concept of, 14
Nauhaus, Walter, 41
Nazi party, 108, 121, 122, 146-47, 168
origins of, 1, 17
Neupert, Karl, 79
new man, concept of, 45, 57-58, 95-96, 113-14
Nietzsche, Friedrich, 105, 113, 132
Nordic mythology, as Nazi influence, 39-40, 49,
78, 80, 145. See also Wotan
number mysticism, 29, 51-52, 135
Nuremberg Trials, 45, 99-100, 151, 154, 160

obedience, as mystic and Nazi task, 34-36,
46-47, 87, 96-97, 98, 107, 108, 109, 112,
152, 155-56, 162, 168
Order of Bektashi Dervishes, 63, 64
Order of New Templars, 5, 17, 19, 47
Order of the Teutonic Knights, 14-15, 85-86
Orientalism, 8-9, 105
Ostara, 5, 17-19, 21
erotic racism in, 18, 47, 105

paganism. See Nordic mythology
Pan-Germanism, 5, 24, 25, 28, 51
Paracelsus, 117, 134
Pauwels, Louis, 64, 65, 66
Payne, Robert, Life and Death of Adolf Hitler,
The, 42
Phelps, Reginald H., "Before Hitler Came:
Thule Society and Germanen Orden," 24,
51-52
Plato, 74-75
Podmore, Frank, From Mesmer to Christian
Science, 117-18
Pohl, Hermann, 24, 25, 26, 27